LIVING WITH
PURPOSE

POSITIVE LIVING PRODUCES POSITIVE RESULTS

MATT DOBSON

Copyright 2020 by author Matt Dobson
Author of Living With Purpose Volume 1, 2, 3, and 4

ISBN— 9798582465300

Camellia House Publishing, Jay, FL

Printed in the United States of America.

TABLE OF CONTENTS

TABLE OF CONTENTS *continued*

TABLE OF CONTENTS *continued*

TABLE OF CONTENTS *continued*

TABLE OF CONTENTS *continued*

I affectionately dedicate this book to my
sweet, loving sister,

Susanna Ranae Dobson;

in life's daily challenges,
she never gives up.

"We know that God causes everything to work together for the good of those who love God and are called according to His purpose for them"
Romans 8:28 NLT

Introduction

The first sentence of the best-selling book of all-time says, "In the beginning God created the heavens and the earth". This means that all of life begins with God and you are a part of His wonderful creation. The air breathed into you was given out of God's good purpose to see you succeed in your endeavors and to glorify Him in your journey. With that positive thought, we can know life is worth living!

While navigating through this world we will be frequently challenged by unexpected traps and hidden snares. A lack of understanding about the abundant life found in Christ can cause serious trouble and sincere questions concerning faith. Therefore, the words and stories of this book are intended to help you prepare for those inevitable challenges and encourage you to not give up your pursuit of the abundant life!

Since God created all things, doesn't it seem wise and proper to give Him first place in our affections, our ambitions, and our actions? Since life is a journey, we need to travel trustingly in His grace. Since living is intended to be our mission, let's live by helping others day to day, following the example of Christ. Since living will sometimes be a battle, we should depend on Him for victory. Since God has loved us so freely, we should obey Him eagerly. And since life is short, may you learn to live with purpose, redeeming the time you have been given by the Creator.

R. Matthew Dobson

January 1, 2020

Jay, Florida

1

Stand Tall Like a Tree

"Stand firm in the faith. Be courageous and strong. And do everything with love"
(1 Corinthians 16:13).

In 1907, President Theodore Roosevelt issued an Arbor Day proclamation to all the school children in the United States. Arbor Day exists to celebrate trees and educate people concerning their importance to our health and the environment. I'm not sure what schools are teaching kids these days concerning the importance of Arbor Day; but it is worth the effort in my opinion.

I recall one day being in an Arbor Day program as a student at Jay Elementary School. After it concluded, the Student Council, along with our sponsor and principal, planted cedar trees on the front lawn. The trees were lined up one beside another and we had a string of 12-13 of them. I was proud of them and felt we had done a civic duty by planting trees in the school yard. My sentimental nerve was touched through the years as I watched them grow. They grew to be fine healthy trees and they became a natural barrier to the busy highway in front of the school. Several years after graduating from high school and college, it saddened me to return one day to see they had been cut down and replaced with a chain-link fence. But that's progress I suppose.

I've always been thankful for my rural upbringing and trees contributed to that gratitude. Growing up in the country I developed an affinity for the great outdoors, especially the woods, the creeks, and the red dirt roads. To this day, as I run or hike through the woodlands of my home town, the trees that surround me seem to be companions and friends to me. I remember when fishing with my grandfather we hiked and waded through the river swamp and came upon a grand stand of tremendous oaks. The acorns were almost as big as golf balls and I can remember standing at the base of the tree and looking up with awe and admiration. It was as if the tree tops grew straight into heaven.

The quaint piece of land my parents purchased as a young family had numerous trees on the property. And there was a certain big oak I was particularly fond of. It stood on the east side of our yard where I would always go on Saturday mornings. I considered it my base camp where I'd make my plans for a full day of adventures. I revisit that tree in my memory and think of the poem, "Woodman, Spare that Tree" written by George Pope Morris:

"When but an idle boy, I sought its grateful shade; In all their gushing joy, here too, my sister play'd; My mother kiss' d me here, my father press' d my hand—forgive this foolish tear but let that old tree stand!"

Trees are usually considered in the Bible as good things and are used as a symbol of plenty. The psalmist says,

"The godly will flourish like palm trees and grow strong like the cedars of Lebanon. Even in old age they will still produce fruit; they'll remain vital and green"
(Psalm 92:12-14).

In Isaiah 55:12-13 it says,

"The trees of the field will clap their hands. Where once there were thorns, cypress trees will grow. Where nettles grow, myrtles will sprout up."

The Lord is always offering to trade with us like that. When we yield to the temptations of the evil one and do wrong things, we become filled with thorns and briars enter our thoughts and conversations. As a result, we become uncomfortable, unpleasant, and hard to live with. But God promises if we will forsake our sins and ask for His help, He'll take away our thorns and briars, and make us like the cypress tree, with its sweet-smelling balsam and its beautiful feathery sprays. He can help our attitudes be more attractive like the myrtle tree with its lily-white flowers and fragrant berries. How strange it is for anyone to refuse such an advantageous bargain like that!

For trees to grow strong and tall they must have plenty of moisture for the root system. The writer of the first Psalm compares the people who delight in the law of the Lord, meditate on His Words day and night, and try to please Him by their conduct. He compares them to a:

"Tree planted along the riverbank, bearing fruit each season. Their leaves never wither, and they prosper in all they do" (Psalm 1:2-3).

Sometimes there's a tree which has every chance yet yields nothing but leaves every year. Jesus told a story about a tree like that, and how the owner of it was discouraged and told the gardener to cut it down and burn it up. But the gardener pleaded for it and said if the master would let it stand another year, he would give the tree special care and see if it would not bear fruit (Luke 13:6-9).

Let's all ask ourselves the serious question, "Do I bear any fruit that's pleasing to Christ?" It is a personal question we can only answer for ourselves. Choose to commit to it, stand tall for Christ. Weather the storms and strong winds that beat against you and in so doing you'll glorify our Father which is in Heaven.

2

Kindred Spirits

*"Rather, we must enjoy having guests in our home and show-
ing hospitality, loving what is good, living wisely, and being
just and devout"*
(Titus 1:8).

A young man who lived many years ago tells the story of his favorite uncle. He says, "When I was a boy and
lived in a farmhouse out in the country it was always a
jolly time when Uncle Wallace came to see us. He was a
preacher and traveled a circuit so large that it took him
four weeks to get around on horseback. We children
were always glad to see Uncle Wallace come, because he
was such a kind-hearted, good man, and was always so
gentle and cheerful that he brought the sunshine with
him. Uncle Wallace knew how to do many things besides
preaching. He could make the best whistles of any man
in the country, and he could take the stalk of an elderber-
ry-tree and make a squirt-gun that would make any country boy's mouth water. He was full of stories that pleased
both the old and the young folks. When he read the Bi-

ble, he did it in such a natural way that it seemed as if he was reading a letter, and when he led at family prayers, we all felt the Lord was not very far away. All the people were glad to have him come, because he brought such a happy, good time along with him".

After reading this testimonial, it reminded me of two stories in the Bible. One was about an old preacher who traveled on a big circuit. His name was Elijah and the story can be found in 1 Kings 17. The Lord had this preacher stay for a long time by the side of a little brook, and the ravens brought him food, and he drank out of the brook. But after a while the brook dried up, and the Lord told him to go to the house of a widow woman who had one son. The woman was very poor, and had only a little food left, but she divided it with the good man. Because she was so kind to him the Lord kept her food from giving out, so that if the preacher stayed, there was plenty to eat.

Like Uncle Wallace, the widow and her little boy thought Elijah was welcome company to have about the house. It's a blessed thing to give a welcome to visitors who bring the Lord with them.

The second story I'm thinking about is when two young men set the "Ark of God" or some call it the "Ark of the Covenant" on an oxcart and drove the oxen along to Jerusalem with it. The story is told in 2 Samuel 6:3-15. The Bible explains when they came to a place where the ground was rough one of the young men took hold of the Ark of God to steady it. And because no one was to touch the Ark of God, he died right there on the spot. And David, who was King at the time, was afraid to have the Ark taken any farther. So, he left it in the house of a man by the name of Obededom, and it stayed there three months. The strange thing about it was that from the moment it was left there, God's blessings was on that house, and all Obededom or his wife, or his boys and his girls did was so successful that the neighbors all talked about it, and David lost his fear of the Ark of God and had the Ark brought up to Jerusalem.

These stories are examples of a great and mighty truth. There's always a good time in the house when Jesus comes to live there. Which leads to the question, "Is Jesus Christ welcome in your house?" Is it any wonder that humankind has tried to kick God out of the school house, court house, and other public places and we have chaos and turmoil in these areas? Even in some church houses, secular influences are introduced and are being welcomed and disguised as being of God. God has standards that have been in place since the beginning of time. Perhaps we have forgotten the great command that we are to have:

"No other gods before Him" (Exodus 20:3).

Christ desires to enter our dwelling places and to bring the good things of life. Jesus says,

"Look I stand at the door and knock. If you hear my voice and open the door, I will come in, and we will share a meal together as friends" (Revelation 3:20).

Good times await the person and families that welcome Jesus into their homes. But he will never force his way in. There must be a willingness; a submission to His invitation. A poem by M.S. Lowndes clearly describes this opportunity: "Here I am standing at the door of your heart, won't you let me come in and flood light where there's dark? For I have been knocking for such a long time, don't leave it much longer to become a child of mine. I just want you to know that I love you so much and can fill your heart within that once was starved of love. So please don't delay in responding to me, for I may not keep knocking and I have not a key. I will never force you to open the door; it's all up to you, my friend, to receive me as Lord".

Christ has promised to come into the heart of any person who invites him. If Jesus is allowed to stay with us, pride, meanness, jealousy, enviousness, bitterness, and hatred will have to leave. Then we can all say, "good riddance to bad rubbish". Let Christ into your life and start experiencing life as he intended it for you. This life will certainly not be without some difficulty. But how abundantly full of peace, love, and joy it will be both now and into eternity.

3

A Shepherd in the Storm

"I am the Good Shepherd. A good shepherd sacrifices his life
for the sheep"
(John 10:11).

While attending an arts festival several years ago I noticed two paintings on large canvases. They were impressive due to their size and intricate details. But it was the contrasting elements that caught my eye the most. They were pictures of sheep. The first one was a summer scene with a beautiful landscape that stretched as far as the eye could see. It was a great restful valley, with a lazy stream winding its peaceful way through the meadow. In the foreground and on the hillside, stood a flock of sheep; some grazing and a few resting. The sun was shining, and the shepherd seemed to be cooling himself under the shade of a tree. A cattle dog was also sitting by the tree; a little more alert than his master. In the whole scene, there wasn't one element of discord to break the harmony of it. My reflective spirit began to murmur the sweet words:

"The Lord is my shepherd; I shall not want, he maketh me to lie down in green pastures; He leadeth me beside the still waters" (Psalm 23:1-2).

There was another painting beside it. Perhaps it had been painted as a companion piece. But I noted it was by a different artist. It was a picture of sheep but had a much different scene. It portrayed a flock of sheep that had been caught out in the pasture in a snowstorm. It wasn't a gentle falling snow, like a feather might fall from a bird in flight. It was what you would imagine a blizzard to be; the wind raging and blowing fiercely. The clouds looked angry. The whirlwinds were piling the snow in banks around a few shrubs and a lonely tree. When you looked closely into the sheep's eyes you could see a look of fear. The shepherd was nowhere to be found on the landscape. Perhaps I thought, he had already perished. But near them were two shepherd dogs. One was a smaller one and he was standing in front of the other with his head between the larger dog's forelegs, trying to escape the cold, bitter slap of the wind. The bigger dog stood there strong and faithful.

Any art enthusiast will tell you, when you view a painting, you imagine what the artist is trying to convey. To me, the position of his stance and the look on the bigger dog's face seemed to say to the poor sheep: "I can't do much for you. No dog could get you home through this awful storm, but I won't desert you. I'll stand by and keep you company and if need be, I will

die with you."

But in the distance the artist revealed the deeper meaning of this picture. A huge wooden cross stood tall with a pile of rocks around its base. I thought to myself, thank God the Cross of Jesus Christ can do more than that for us! We all come into this world as poor lost sinners, and often go astray like these poor sheep lost in the storm. But Christ didn't leave lofty Heaven, where he enjoyed eternal joy, and tell us: "I can't do much for you. I don't know how to get you out of the storm and bring you back to your heavenly home. I'm sorry and I'll stay here with you, and if I can't do anything else, I'll die with you." That would be a heroic narrative from Jesus at best, wouldn't it?

But Jesus did a much better thing for us. He was rich and yet for our sakes, he became poor, and gave his life not that he might die with us only, but that he died for us, and bore our sins in his own body on the Cross. Jesus says,

"I am the Good Shepherd; I know my own sheep and they know me, just as my Father knows me and I know the Father. So, I sacrifice my life for the sheep"
(John 10:14-15).

Are you in his flock? Can you be counted as one of God's children? Embrace God and His wonderful love. In the most fearful storms you must face, His love will save your life!

4

Peace Comes When Sharing the Good News

"How can they hear about him unless someone tells them? And how will anyone go and tell them without being sent? That is why the Scriptures say, how beautiful are the feet of messengers who bring good news!"
(Romans 10:14-15).

While serving as a U.S. Army Reserve Battalion Chaplain in Jackson, Mississippi I spent part of an early morning going over my notes for chapel service. I read a passage from the Gospel of Matthew where it says,

"Jesus reached out and touched a man" that was in need and the man was instantly healed (Matthew 8:3).

The Master's touch brought healing and peace to the poor leper.

Peace comes to us in many ways, as it did for this man. I've known about God's peace since I was a child. I felt peace when I got out of my car that day and heard a mockingbird welcoming the morning with a melodious tune. I paused, listened for a few seconds, and agreed with my little feathered friend, it was going to be a wonderful day.

When our unit broke for lunch, I visited a fast food restaurant and walked swiftly across the parking lot because I was hungry. As I stepped up to the side entrance door, I heard someone say, "Sir, hello sir!" I turned and saw a man, sitting in his car with his window down waiting in the drive-thru line.

I responded by saying, "How are you?"

He didn't motion for me, but I sensed he wanted to talk. I cautiously walked over to the driver's window and he said, "I noticed you're in an army uniform. I'm so excited and wanted to tell you. You see, I tailor suits and uniforms. I went into business for myself and have been trying to take my services on base at Camp Shelby near Hattiesburg. I just got word last week, they have approved my business and I'll start next week. I'm nervous about the whole deal and want to make sure I do a good job and they will keep me. I see the cross on your uniform, and I know you're a chaplain. Will you pray for me?"

After telling him congratulations I assured him I would pray for him. At that split second, a voice spoke to me and said, "Do it now. Pray with him and give him some of the peace you got from the mockingbird this morning."

I recognized the voice. It was God's Spirit speaking to

me. I reached to shake the gentleman's hand and said, "Let's pray right now. There's no better time than the present."

I thanked God for giving this man his new job, and I prayed God would prosper him using his gifts and abilities. I prayed that his hands would help serve others. After a short goodbye. He said, "Chaplain, one more thing. Here's my business card. Look me up when you train at Camp Shelby sometime."

I looked at the card and it said, "The Master's Touch", Sewing with Passion, William J. Pope. 30 Years' Experience".

Meeting this man was one of many Divine appointments in my life. It was personally significant because a few hours prior I had been reading about Jesus' healing touch, the Master's Touch. Jesus' touch has been healing and giving peace since the beginning of all time.

We all seek peace. Because there's a malicious enemy in the devil, who will do all he can within the powers of hell to disappoint us, defeat us, and destroy our witness for Jesus Christ. If you live under the illusion that you don't have an enemy in the world, you need to cause that illusion to evaporate. The devil is alive and out to get you and will do so unless you commit yourself without reservation to the Lordship of Jesus Christ. The Christian life is a struggle. It's like running uphill, like swimming upstream. Followers of Christ are not to float through life.

Ephesians 6:15 tells us,

"To put on the sandals (shoes) of the gospel of peace that comes from the Good News so that you will be fully prepared."

We should not be dogmatic about the meaning of this verse. It has to do with the gospel that brings the peace of God into the hearts of people, and it specifically emphasizes an attitude of readiness and eagerness. Perhaps what the apostle Paul was trying to communicate is that if we are to overcome evil, and life's anxieties, we must respond to God's goodness and let peace fill our hearts. We must also have a deep inward eagerness to share the message that brings peace and joy to the hearts and lives of others that we encounter.

The prophet Isaiah declared Jesus as:

"The Prince of Peace" (Isaiah 9:6).

Jesus came to bring peace to people and among people. The peace he seeks to give is not that which is born on the battlefield but found in the depths of the human heart. His peace is not the peace of stagnation or inactivity. His peace is not a spiritual narcotic to keep one from facing reality. The Prince of Peace gives believers peace with God through a right relationship with Him.

Using sandals of a Roman soldier as a metaphor, Paul

declared that if we are to overcome evil, we must have our feet prepared, that is, we must be eager and ready—to carry Christ's message of peace to all who are in spiritual darkness. Isaiah 52:7 proclaims the following:

"How beautiful on the mountains are the feet of the messenger who brings good news, the good news of peace and salvation, the news that the God of Israel reigns!"

The primary emphasis of this passage is on the proclamation of the good news of God's love to a needy world. The subjective effect of this attitude of readiness will provide for us as individuals the protection we need from Satan who wants to rob you of peace. May you be able to respond to God's call as did Isaiah, "Here am I! Send me." We need to go everywhere announcing the good news of God's love.

5

Happiness Comes from the Heart

"A glad heart makes a happy face"
(Proverbs 15:13).

A little girl admired her Daddy for many reasons. And one of them was his consistent display of happiness and positive attitudes. "Why are you so happy all the time Daddy?" she asked.

Realizing the teachable moment, he told her, "It's because of Jesus! He's the one that makes me happy. It's because of how much he loves us!"

"I want to be happy like that too!" she exclaimed.

It wasn't very long after that conversation this little girl accepted Jesus as her Savior and she became a happy Christian. It's true, Christ makes all the difference and gives us the greatest reason to be filled with joy.

All other things being equal, a cheerful person, who is good humored with themselves as well as with other folks, will succeed better than the one who's selfish and down-in-the-dumps. For the Bible says,

"A cheerful heart is good medicine" (Proverbs 17:22).

You will not get genuine laughter or sincere smiles out of a person unless they have a cheerful heart. The kind of laughter that makes people healthy and the kind that is longed for is the kind that springs from a truly happy person.

The way to happiness and to enjoy its life-giving energy is to pursue God and His Son Jesus Christ. Jesus' own words were,

"I have come so that you may have an abundant (joyful) life" (John 10:10).

And Proverbs 15:15 reminds us,

"For the happy heart; life is a continual feast."

If a person is selfish and they have an angry spirit within, there's not much of anything that'll make them happy. Usually these people have trouble making friends and there's not too many that care to spend time with someone who's mad, full of hate, and treats others with disrespect. But if the heart of a person is high-spirited and jolly, then everyone else will get a sunny tinge from being near them and listening to their good humor.

Have you ever noticed how different things look on a cloudy, dark day, than on a day that's full of sunshine and warmth? The sunshine coming from the sky sparkles on the water and it makes the colors of the garden come alive with energy and brilliance. The trees and flowers reach upward to grab some of it themselves. So, a person's spirit, the condition of their heart, changes the appearance of everybody and everything it encounters.

King Solomon says,

"A glad heart makes a happy face" (Proverbs 15:13).

And that kind of countenance is very attractive. Start your day by smiling at the first person you meet, and you'll automatically impact their behavior. A smile is the simplest and easiest way to make a positive difference in someone's life. Give them a smile or an encouraging word and your happy spirit will make them happier as a result. This is called "spreading cheer" and it gives you the bright title of "spirit lifter".

Don't think for a moment this is not important; for it is. All through life you'll find that the light-hearted person, whose laughter is spontaneous, gushes out of them like a fresh spring leaping out from under a rock on a hillside. These people have a greater advantage in any profession, social setting, or circumstance than the person who's negative, sour, gloomy, and selfish. Most people know a good thing when they see it. And most people can sense a positive person because they tend to build others up, rather than put people down. People give preference to the person who makes them smile over the person whose glum and makes them want to walk in the other direction.

A man was having his picture taken and the photographer told him that if he didn't cheer up and smile, the picture would be ugly.

The man said, "When I feel ugly inside, I don't look pretty on the outside."

But there's a cure for this! Three simple rules, when followed, can help you get a laughing spirit. And the more of it you have and the more you use it, the better chance it will become a permanent part of your own personality. You'll never develop it as a part of who you are until you first gain the spirit of it.

The first step is that you get in the habit of doing the right things. If a person feels they've done something wrong, the wrong will haunt them and chase the smiles away. If you know you've done wrong, repent of it at once; ask God to forgive, and if it's a wrong against anybody else, go straight to the person, confess your wrong, and ask forgiveness. When you've done everything that you can do to make it right, you'll be astonished to notice how the load will be lifted off your heart and how happy it will be again.

The second step is to never hold a grudge against anybody. If you were to hang a big dark blanket over a window in your home, it would keep the sunshine from entering. A grudge acts the same way. It keeps the joy and happiness from shining through a person's life. Grudges and resentment have a powerful effect on a person's action toward other people. The aura surrounding a person is a strong indicator of what's in their heart. Frances Hodgson Burnett once wrote, "Where you tend a rose, a thistle cannot grow." If anybody does you wrong, forgive them, and try to make peace with them, for that's the way to happiness.

The third and final rule is the surest ingredient for happiness—try to do some kind deed for someone else every day; not once a week, but every day do something to add to their happiness. The pleasure you give them will somehow find its way back into your heart and give you as much cheer as it does for the one whom you have been kind.

<u>Recipe for Continued Happiness</u>

- ♦ Do the right things.
- ♦ Never hold a grudge against someone.
- ♦ Do someone a kind deed every day.

6

Fixing Yourself on the Inside

"Anyone who belongs to Christ has become a new person. The old life is gone; a new life has begun!"
(2 Corinthians 5:17).

It's troubling that so many people live in a restless and disparaging condition. Countless people are dissatisfied with life in general and the slightest petty annoyances set them off. Even more troubling is the inability for the average person to sit still for any length of time. Being still and silent are strange and unfamiliar states that today's culture doesn't seem to appreciate. Our hyped-up society goes from one swinging vine to the next.

The disturbing trend is that people are getting high on drugs and forming addictions to painkillers and recreational drugs. I've known several people, young and old, rich and poor who have died as a result of an accumulation of these in their body. I'm in no way passing judgement upon them but have seen too many lives wasted on quick fixes and bad trips that are taken to escape reality. And I repeat, it's not just the poor or low-income individuals that are plagued by this problem.

A police officer in a big city found the following handwritten note by the dead body of a young lady who died of a drug overdose: "Illicit drugs are my shepherds I shall always want. They maketh me to lie down in gutters, they leadeth me beside the troubled waters. They destroyeth my soul. They leadeth me in the paths of wickedness. Yea, I shall walk through the valley of poverty in spirit and will fear all evil. For thou art with me—my drugs. The needles and capsules try to comfort me. Thou robbest my head of reason. My cup runneth over with sorrow. Surely my drug addiction shall stalk me all the days of my life. And I will dwell in the house of the dead forever. Truly this is my psalm. I want to quit, but jail didn't cure me, the hospital didn't help me for long. How did this happen? How did I get off track with life? Why am I here? Is there an answer to life's trouble?"

If there's one positive thing I can say for this poor girl, she is honest. When is the last time you were honest with yourself? When is the last time you analyzed yourself? When is the last time you took a good honest look in the mirror? One of the most painful things in the world is to accept the truth about yourself.

There are people who have made it materially, but they

are empty on the inside. The problem with people who seek drugs as their answer to life's dullness is that this answer will never solve the problem. Grant it, the world is in a chaotic state. People want to get hold of something to fill their emptiness, but also speak to the everyday pressures of their business life, family relationships, and how to deal with their children.

Don't let your feelings of dissatisfaction or distraction from what's important in life take hold of you and lead you by the hand to some dead-end street or dreaded habit. You have a free will, and God has made you. If you're completely honest with yourself, you can begin to deal with those things that are making you feel dissatisfied. Illicit drugs can never help you, but honesty sure can.

Decide not to live a life dependent on a pill or a drink. Accept and believe in a value system that says you're worth more than that. Perhaps the values set forth in God's Word have not been taught to you or maybe they've been forgotten because of the culture's distractions. Your hope for better days will not disappoint you and help does exist for those who want it! If parents want to help their kids steer free from the traps of drugs and society's cesspool of smut, there needs to be a continuity within the family. A consistent message of hope and love that comes from a relationship with Christ. There's a spiritual answer for all things.

Jesus said,

"My purpose is to give them an abundant and satisfying life" (John 10:10).

If people would accept Jesus as their ruler and guide of their life, they would find happiness and fulfillment in this life. You mustn't wait until you've cleaned up your life before coming to him—he'll take care of you. Jesus' presence in a person's life will cast out the failure elements in their personalities. Jesus has the power to cast out the demons in our life just as he did for others years ago (Luke 8:2).

One of Jesus' promises:

"I am with you always, even to the end of the age" (Matthew 28:20),

means that the abundant life is never ending. Stresses and disappointments will come. And never underestimate the human error element in us. We have a mistake tendency, but Christ never makes mistakes. You reduce your mistake tendency when you stay close to him.

Consider the fact we are led by our thought process. That is another powerful reason not to distort our thinking with some drug fix. We need to think clearly. Our emotions are also at risk when under the influence of drugs or alcohol. An emotion can run wild and take us along with it. When it does, that's when we start reaching out to

things like drugs. Don't let illicit drugs control you anymore. Ask for help. Find someone who will listen to your story and let them help you. But the first thing is to ask God to help you overcome your temptation. There is no chemical solution to a spiritual problem.

Ask God to forgive you for your shortcomings, and He will (1 John 1:9). And then decide to live in that forgiveness, rather than continuing to live in your faults. Your life is far more important than you might realize. You are somebody, created in the image of God to be somebody. You'll never be happy until you start being what you were born to be. You would've never been born if there wasn't some good in your being here. Go on the adventure of your life with God and let Him remake you, energize you, and make your life count!

7

Birds Don't Worry, Why Should You?

"Don't worry about things. Seek God and He will give you what you need. Don't worry about tomorrow"
(Matthew 6:31-34).

Early in our marriage, my wife and I purchased a house that was listed on the National Registry of Historical Places. It was built in 1901 in a small town in the northwest corner of Florida. We both had an affinity for old homes and this seemed like a grand opportunity to restore and preserve a small part of history. With research, we found that the original owner had been an avid bird-watcher. So much was her love of birds; she had the small acreage on which the house stood, certified as a National Bird Sanctuary. There were blue berry bushes planted in all the corners of the yard, numerous camellia shrubs and trees in which the birds could build their nests. Bird houses still stand so that our feathered friends can find shelter and sanctuary year after year. We also learned her house maids would bake cornbread each morning to feed the birds. We were also given her half-century old journal that noted the birds she observed every day for an entire year (1958). Naturally, when the subject of birds is mentioned, we think of this old home place.

Jesus was, and still is the master teacher. While not always easy to understand, he often spoke in parables. His stories are relatable to everyday life and his lessons are practical enough to be lived by each of us. But these parables also make you think; to the point where you're challenged to believe more, to exercise your faith more, and to trust more despite what you may be feeling or can see now.

His teaching in Matthew 6:25-34 gives the cure for anxiety. Matthew 6:26-27 says,

"Look at the birds, they don't plant seeds, gather a harvest and put it in barns; yet your Father in heaven takes care of them! Aren't you worth more than birds? Can any of you live a bit longer by worrying about it?"

This whole passage is an antidote to worry. To worry is a persistent temptation and struggle for many people. We are presented a beautiful analogy between God's care for the birds and His care for us. We've asked the question, "Aren't you worth more than the birds (the lesser)?"

God's promises are to take care of His obedient people (the greater).

God commands us not to worry, but some may ask how that's possible considering all the trouble in this world. The following 5 things are God's cure for W-O-R-R-Y:

Many people try to avoid work. However, **WORK** is an effective antidote to worry. It's difficult to worry and work at the same time. Doing God's work is even more helpful. When we're concerned about the problems of others and we try to give them genuine assistance, we tend to forget our own problems.

Secondly, people often think negative to their own detriment. The worse-case scenario rarely happens, but if that's all we think about then the chances are greater it will. The struggle with thoughts of self-doubt and self-deprecation, are a real struggle for those worrying how they're going to make it. We must counter the negative by being **OPTIMISTIC** and practice positive thinking, counting our blessings and "naming them one-by-one". Make it a practice to look for the good, instead of the bad.

Thirdly, don't be the person who solely relies on others, rather than God. People will let you down, God never will. **RELIANCE** upon and showing appreciation for those who help us is a mark of a Christian, but our ultimate trust and thanks needs to be in God. Hebrews 13:5 says,

"For God has said, I will never leave you, I will never aban-don you."

God is the One that never fails.

Fourthly, Nehemiah 8:10 is a sharp reminder of what our relationship with God offers:

"Don't be dejected and sad, for the joy of the Lord is your strength."

It's impossible to rejoice and worry at the same time. We must claim the joy that can be ours. *REJOICING* in the Lord is part of the worry cure.

Finally, we must *YIELD* ourselves to God. Even in Jesus' most excruciating hour on the Cross, he prayerfully yielded to his Father's will. We must do the same. To do so is to follow a guaranteed formula to cure the worry habit. Work, optimism, reliance, and rejoicing will eliminate worry from our lives when we yield to God's will.

Instead of worrying, Jesus says in the passage of Matthew 6, we should not worry about all the necessities of life. "Instead be concerned above everything else with the Kingdom of God and with what He requires of you, and He will provide you with all these things. So, don't worry about tomorrow. There's no need to add to the troubles each day brings."

Worry seems so reasonable. For some, it may seem to be necessary. But it's not, according to Jesus. Will we believe him? Are you willing and prepared to live a worry-free life of trusting God to take care of you? Sometimes a little bird-watching is fun and can be good for our faith. Let the birds remind you of God's promises.

<u>God's Cure for Worry</u>

W-ork

O-ptimism

R-eliance

R-ejoicing

Y-ield

8

Small Steps Lead to Big Encouragement

"That is why we never give up. Though our bodies are dying,
our spirits are being renewed every day"
(2 Corinthians 4:16).

There's hardly anything more motivating than to see a person take a physical challenge or limitation and maximize its positive effectiveness. There once was a man in the church where I pastored who had a condition that confined him to the use of a walker. He could only take small steps.

After talking with him about his underlying medical condition, he said, "You know I don't see my problem as a hindrance, I see it as a way to exercise my faith and witness."

"You're a strong person and God will honor that kind of attitude," I responded.

"I'm slow, but I get there, eventually. As my condition worsened I sought physical therapy. I surprised them by how much progress I made in a short period of time." He let go of his walker and said, "Watch this!" Much to my surprise, he grabbed the back of the first church pew, took a step, then another, then another, and with a consistent effort made it all the way to the altar.

"That's fantastic!" I exclaimed.

He said, "Yep, I'm a winner. And let me tell you something else. A doctor who treats other patients with my condition was impressed with my will-power and asked if I would speak to one of her patients who was depressed and cast down. When I met the lady, she was sad and perplexed. She didn't know me, but I said I know what you're going through. I'm in it now too but look at me! I can drive, I'm enrolled in college, and doing the best I could hope for. After some more talk, she said I helped her and pulled her out of the depths of despair. It made me feel good that I could help somebody that's suffering. That's what we should do, help one another. We can all be on the winning side."

As I age and continue to run for fitness and fun, I'll have an occasional ache and pain. I am tempted to lean toward self-pity because I'm slower than I used to be. But then, the Spirit reminds me of my friend, and my pity turns to praise. God blesses His children in different ways and we must be grateful for what abilities we do have—great or small. Without Christ we're all doomed to a life of heartache with no hope beyond this earth. As Christians, we have no reason to be defeated within our spirit. 2 Corinthians 4:8-10 says,

"We are troubled on every side, yet not distressed. We're perplexed, but not in despair. Persecuted, but not forsaken by God; cast down, but not destroyed. Through suffering, our bodies continue to share in the death of Jesus so that the life of Jesus may also be seen in our bodies."

Christians are destined for Heaven and eternal joy. What we must do on earth is survive as best we can until God gives us relief from our labor and calls us home. The Bible says,

"We belong to Him; the power of the life-giving Spirit frees us from the power of sin. Christ lives in us and despite trouble, threat of death, and all of life's sorrows, overwhelming victory is ours through Christ, who loves us" (Romans 8).

If you're a Christian, you maybe "troubled—but you're not destroyed." Christians have troubles, but they have One to whom they can go and depend upon. We need not be distressed. God can and will replace our worry and strain with His peace and rest.

If you're a Christian, you may be "perplexed—but you're not in despair". It seems one problem follows on the heels of other problems. You're not alone; millions of people are frustrated, confused, and perplexed. While multitudes of people are losing hope and giving into drugs and drinks, your hope is still in God (Psalm 42:11). He never fails and the best is yet to come.

If you're a Christian, you may be "persecuted—but you're not deserted." Persecution has been around for centuries and can come in the form of abusive treatment, silence, neglect, lies, and more subtle ways. This is the time to trust God, who will never leave you and says you're more than a conqueror (Romans 8:37).

If you're a Christian, you may be "cast down—but you're not destroyed." A dedicated and disciplined Christian must be willing to suffer "for Jesus' sake", knowing that:

"If we suffer, we shall also reign with him"
(2 Tim. 2:12).

If you're cast down, look up to God in hope and remember faithfulness to God brings victory both now and eternally.

Take your troubles, look at your challenges, and see what they can teach you. Then find someone who needs to hear from you. If you're saved, you're on the winning side and it's your duty to help make more winners. When you do, you're making a difference in someone's eternity.

Now that's Kingdom Building and that's the sweetest victory of all.

<u>The Mindset of a Winner</u>

- Troubled—but you're not destroyed.

- Perplexed—but you're not in despair.

- Persecuted—but you're not deserted.

- Cast down—but you're not destroyed.

9

Let Others See Christ in You

*"Just as God raised Christ from the dead, He will give life to
your mortal bodies by the same Spirit living
within you"*
(Romans 8:11).

I once had the humbling opportunity to lead a worship service (chapel) for a group of military service members just weeks before they were to deploy to a foreign country. I had served as their chaplain for a 3-week training rotation at the National Training Center (NTC). Many of the Soldiers were tired and longed to enjoy the comforts of home and see their loved ones one more time before they left for their mission. I can assure you I knew the importance of this moment and my duty to share some parting words with them.

Last words are important. Whether it's a husband being shipped overseas to war, or the mother of two children going to serve her country in a foreign land, or even a coach's pregame speech before taking the field, last words are often the thing that people hold on to and reflect upon as they try to push forward in life. They frequently represent something important, and they're usually something you don't forget.

Jesus' last recorded words on earth are found in Matthew 28:18-20. They explain what his followers are to do in the period between his first coming and his second coming. What he said to his disciples, known as the Great Commission, represented something so profound that it enabled all Christians to have the privilege of building the Kingdom for all eternity. The last words Jesus spoke on a Galilean hill-side, became the marching orders for all Soldiers of God. That day, Jesus Christ wanted the disciples, that day to focus on the mission, and pass it on. So that all who would follow would know that his power and presence would go with them.

The final words I gave to these deploying units at NTC were four simple points on how Christians should live. Many people profess to be Christians but fail to live the Christian life as spelled out in God's Army. There is a step-by-step plan in how to practice what we profess.

The first step is to live *IN* Christ. The Scripture is very clear in 2 Corinthians 5:17,

"If any person be in Christ, they are a new creation."

Their sins are forgiven, and their guilt has been removed. They are new creatures in Christ. Old things have passed away and everything is new. The Spirit of God comes into a person's life and cleanses them, renews them, and gives them the Spirit of God's love. They become alive in Christ. We can't possibly clean up our lives by ourselves, and it's impossible to let anyone else "fix" us to be presented to God. When we surrender to the promptings of God's Holy Spirit, He assumes the responsibility of giving us the power to overcome our sin. Those who live in Christ are directed by the Holy Spirit and strengthened for the challenges of each day.

The second step is to live **LIKE** Christ. A popular question we can ask ourselves is "what would Jesus do" (WWJD)? Christ's followers have Jesus' example to follow in thinking, hearing, seeing, speaking, doing, and going. Jesus prayed often, was kind, compassionate, and understanding. Practicing daily prayer, Bible reading, exercising faith, loving others, feeding the hungry, caring for the sick, comforting the bereaved—all these help Christians become like Christ. 1 Peter 2:21 says,

"God called you, for Christ himself suffered for you and left you an example, so that you would follow in his steps."

The third step is to live **FOR** Christ. We know that good Soldiers live and sometimes die for their country. They endure hardships, sacrifice ease and pleasure to protect their land and those he or she loves. As a good Soldier of God, we must be ready to perform the 3 "S's" of a good Soldier: Service, Sacrifice, and suffering. Christ gave his life for us. We must do the same for him. We do this by literally denying self and giving him control of our time, talent, and treasure.

"We are ambassadors for Christ" (2 Cor. 5:20).

The fourth and final step is to live **WITH** Christ. Christ is with Christians in this life and in the life to come. Christ has promised to come again and receive us to himself, that where he is there we shall be also (John 14:1-3). What a privilege it is to have the blessed assurance that we can walk daily in this physical life with God's Spirit and have Christ, God's Son, usher us into heaven at God's appointed time. Hallelujah! 1 Thessalonians 4:17 says,

"We will be gathered up along with them (redeemed loved ones) in the clouds to meet the Lord in the air. And so, we will always be with the Lord."

Jesus has given us, the incredible responsibility to be his representatives in the world, to carry his message of love and peace to a world that is broken. That is why we need to know how Christians should live. As we go about telling others what good things God has done for us, we point people to Jesus Christ our Savior. We become the salt and light in our world. Jesus' final words become our words. His message becomes our message. Isn't it amazing, Jesus allows us to share in spreading his gospel? No higher calling or greater privilege exists.

<u>How to Practice What We Profess</u>

- ♦ Live IN Christ.
- ♦ Live LIKE Christ.
- ♦ Live FOR Christ.
- ♦ Live WITH Christ.

10

Make Every Day a Day of Prayer

"When I think of all this, I fall to my knees and pray to the
Father"
(Ephesians 3:14).

Our nation recognizes the first Thursday in the month of May as the National Day of Prayer. The faithful who ardently believe in the power of prayer attend community and local gatherings to give emphasis to this important part of the Christian faith. How committed are you to a viable life of prayer? Everyday should be a day of prayer in the life of a believer.

One of the effects of sin in our life is to keep us from feeling compelled to pray. Satan wants it this way. It's important to understand perfect moral behavior is not a condition for prayer. Don't let guilty feelings over sin keep you from a close relationship with God. He's ready to hear from you and restore you to a right relationship.

I believe if every person would realize the power associated with prayer and start practicing it, there would be less anxiety-ridden people walking around and significantly less people on medication for stress-related issues.

The practice of prayer is the key to spiritually-managing what is important to you. The biblical priest Ezra writes,

"I gave orders for all of us to fast and humble ourselves before our God. We prayed that He would give us a safe journey and protect us, our children, and our goods as we traveled. So, we fasted and earnestly prayed that our God would take care of us, and He heard our prayer" (Ezra 8:21-23).

Ezra knew God's promises to protect His people, but He didn't take them for granted. Ezra said they prayed "earnestly". Too often we pray superficially. Serious prayer requires concentration. It puts us in touch with God's will and it can change us. I once heard that without serious prayer, we reduce God to a quick-service pharmacist with painkillers for our every ailment.

In John 17 Jesus didn't ask God to take believers out of the world or to remove all hindrances from their life, but instead to use them in the world. Since Christ sends us out to the utter-most parts of the earth, we should not try to escape from the world, nor should we avoid all relationships with non-believers. Christians are to be "salt and light" (Matthew 5:13-16) and we are to do the work that God sent us to do.

Because the world is in spiritual warfare where the forces under Satan's power do battle with those under God's authority, we need to protect ourselves. Satan and his forces are motivated by their hatred for Christ and his followers. Jesus prays for us, that God would keep us safe from Satan's power, setting you and me apart, making us holy and pure, and uniting us with his truth (John:11-21). Although Jesus has prayed for our protection, we must be diligent in doing our part by staying spiritually strong through prayer and a conscious application of putting on our spiritual armor (Ephesians 6:10-18). Prayer prepares us for battle. It's been said that "preparation precedes public performance". The same can be said about private performance. The Bible makes it very clear that we're to be on guard, alert, and ready (1 Peter 5:8).

The essence of prayer is not public style, but involves private, personal, communication with God. There's a place for public prayer, but to pray with the intent to impress or where others will notice you, indicates that your real audience is not God.

Finally, when considering our prayer life, we should always pray for one another. Colossians 1:3-4 says,

"We always pray for you, and we give thanks to God, the Father of our Lord Jesus Christ. For we have heard of your faith in Christ Jesus and your love for all of God's people."

When you don't know how to pray for someone use the following thoughts:

Pray that they 1) understand God's will, 2) seek spiritual discernment, 3) honor God, 4) bear good fruit, 5) grow in their knowledge of God, 6) be filled with God's strength, 7) have endurance and patience, 8) stay full of Christ's joy, 9) help others, and 10) always, always give thanks.

All believers have these same basic needs. God welcomes your honest prayers and wants you to express your true feelings to Him. We can do so, because He promises to love us with an everlasting love.

11

The Peace that Comes with Death

"Jesus told her, I am the resurrection and the life. Anyone who believes in me will live, even after dying. Everyone who lives in me and believes in me will never ever die"
(John 11:25-26).

American Country music singer and songwriter Joey Feek was a loving, faithful, Christian woman with many talents. She passed away after a hard-fought battle with cancer. I heard her in an interview four months before her death where she said, "When the doctors told me how bad it was and that my cancer was terminal, I went home, and I cried. But the tears were not because of self-pity, but for my little girl (Indiana Boon Feek was a year-old at the time). I was heartbroken because what affect this would have on her."

Death or the prediction of it can shake the world of those who face it. Joey was a Christian who was grounded in her faith. She knew where she was going and what the future held for her. This gave her peace and security, but she was concerned for her daughter.

I read of a touching incident that happened many years ago. A newspaper published a story about a family consisting of a husband, wife, and a little boy. The mother was stricken with a disease that was going to take her life. It was sudden and dreadful. When the family physician called them together in his solemn, professional way and made known to them the brevity of her prognosis, all their hope sank to the bottom of their hearts. Then the question was posed by one of them, "Who's going to tell her?" They felt it was not the doctor's place, not the aged mother, and the young husband was distraught and walking the floor with clinched hands and a rebellious heart. So, who was to tell her? The aunts and uncles did not want to do it, so the little boy was the only one left.

With no warning, the little boy dropped his book and asked them plainly, "Is Momma going to die?"

Without waiting for an answer, he ran to his mother's room as fast as his feet would carry him. Some friends were already in the room by his sick mother's bedside. They noticed the boy's face was pale as he climbed on the bed and laid his head on his mother's pillow.

"Momma?" he asked sweetly, "Are you afraid to die?"

The woman looked at him and knew why he had asked her this question. Perhaps she had already been thinking about it.

"Who told you Charlie?" she asked faintly.

"Doctor, Papa, and Gamma-everybody," he whispered, "Momma, Momma are you afraid of dying?"

"No Charlie," said the young mother, thinking of her son's sensitive nature, "No, momma won't be afraid."

Remembering what his Sunday School teacher told him about Heaven, he said, "Just shut your eyes in the dark Momma. Keep holding my hand, and when you open them Momma, it'll all be light there."

When the rest of the family made it to the bedside and the young mother fell into a coma, little Charlie held up his hand and said, "Hush! Momma's going to sleep. She won't wake up here anymore."

There was no heart-rendered farewell, no agony of parting. For when the young mother passed, as little Charlie said, "She was in the light."

It is imperative for the person who faces death to come clean. The Bible says,

> **"Each person is destined to die once (physically) and after that comes judgement" (Hebrews 9:27).**

All of us are sinful and prone to error. Therefore, God has made it possible for us to be ready when it comes our time to die. God in His love and forgiveness will not hesitate to cleanse the dirt and stains that come with the bitter warfare of temptation and sin. The following verse can be our testimony:

"I waited patiently for the Lord to help me, and He turned to me and heard my cry. He lifted me out of the pit of despair, out of the mud and the mire. He set my feet on solid ground and steadied me as I walked along. Many will see what He has done and be amazed. They will put their trust in the Lord" (Psalm 40:1-3).

The dying Christian can face death with peace, because the Lord and Savior Jesus Christ has given it to them.

"I am leaving you with a gift, peace of mind and heart. And the peace I give is a gift the world cannot give. So, don't be troubled or afraid" (John 14:27).

When a Christian enters the blessed hope of Heaven, peace forever more becomes their eternal dwelling place.

12

You Were Made for the Mountains

"In the last days, the mountain of the Lord's house will be the highest of all—the most important place on earth. Come, let us go up to the mountain of the Lord. There He will teach us His ways, and we will walk in His paths"
(Isaiah 2:2-3).

Many years ago, I entered the so-called "real world" of professional employment. I was fresh out of graduate school and hired as a director of a YMCA in a small Alabama town. Attending a leadership and certification conference was the first directive given to me by my supervisor. This program school was held in the quaint high-country town of Black Mountain, North Carolina.

My week-long training at the YMCA Blue Ridge Assembly was a "literal" mountaintop experience. The distance of the Black Mountain range, as the crow flies, is only 15 miles, but within these fifteen miles are 18 peaks climbing to at least 6,300 feet. Black Mountain is a sister peak to Mount Mitchell in the heart of the beautiful Blue Ridge Mountains. My YMCA training turned into a spiritual milestone in my life, for it was then that I received clarity concerning my call to Christian ministry. Ever since, Black Mountain has held a special place in my heart. Not only that, the Baptist training and retreat facility called Ridgecrest is where I've also received training. It's only a few miles down interstate 40 and encompasses the same mountain range.

I purposely return year after year for business and pleasure. After every visit, I leave refreshed and Spirit-filled. I believe that as Christians we are made for the mountains. Jesus sought time alone with God in the mountains. This is where Jesus communed with God and learned of God's will and received strength. Matthew 14:23 says,

"After he (Jesus) dismissed them, he went up on a mountainside by himself to pray."

And again, in Luke 6:12,

"One of those days Jesus went out to a mountainside to pray and spent the night praying to God."

Other Scriptures that note his retreat to solitude for prayer are found in Mark 1:35 and Mark 6:46.

It's within the hills you find mountaintops and valleys. Both characterize the life of every person. Most all our experiences fit into these two categories. When I sit on the steps of the YMCA lecture hall at Blue Ridge, I feel as though I'm looking up to the throne room of Heaven. Learning to overcome life's greatest struggles is found in God's throne room. Jesus said,

"Those who are victorious will sit with me on my throne, just as I was victorious and sat with my Father on His throne" (Revelation 3:21).

How wonderful it would be to stay on the mountaintop and bask in divine glory! But discipleship means denying self, taking up a cross, and following Christ, and you can't do that and selfishly stay on the mount of glory.

On a recent visit to Black Mountain, I read the following Scripture while overlooking God's great and marvelous creation:

"Before the mountains were born, before You gave birth to the earth and the whole world, from beginning to end, You are God" (Psalm 90:2).

This magnificent view, along with God's Word, inspired me with 5 powerful truths that can enable any person to overcome life's difficulties and come out a winner:

First, you must ***Prevail in Prayer***. Christ portrayed the example of spending time alone with God in prayer. And you don't have to be in the mountains to do it. You can pray anywhere! All our victories begin with prayer. Every failure and sin can be forgiven by asking God's pardon. All our trials and troubles may be taken to God and left with Him. At the moment of your most burdensome testing's, the wisest thing to do is to run to God's throne room. Like the mountains, God's throne is majestic, strong, and firmly established. Psalm 65:3-6 says,

"Though we are overwhelmed by our sins, You forgive them all. What joy for those You choose to bring near, those who live in Your holy courts. You faithfully answer our prayers with awesome deeds, Oh God our Savior. You're the hope of everyone on earth, even those who sail on distant seas. You formed the mountains by Your power and armed Yourself with mighty strength."

Next, you must ***Pursue the Promises***. God's promises are given for our salvation and his divine help in making it through our time on earth. They're also given for our learning. Like training for your professional development, God's promises, when claimed as our own, can disciple us so that we can find God's will, instructions, and guidance. All of which helps us grow in our personal spiritual development.

Thirdly, we must ***Persist in Patience***. Most of us don't have all the patience we need. God sometimes allows troubles and trials to come so our patience can increase. We learn patience by waiting on God. Some of the biggest trees in the South are found in the forests of the mountains. I can assure you, it takes time for an oak to grow or a pine to stretch above the landscape (Hebrews 10:36).

The next truth to help us overcome is to **Proclaim His Praise**. Psalm 150:6 reads, "Let everything that breaths, sing praises to the Lord." God hears our praise. It often moves His Spirit to act when nothing else can, and it enables us to overcome.

Finally, we must **Promote His Purpose**. We do this best when we witness to the lost and seek to bring them to a saving knowledge of Jesus Christ. We promote God's purposes when we faithfully serve Him with our time, talent, and treasure. We overcome by working for God.

Whatever your state in life---whether it's on a mountaintop or in a valley, know that God's throne is majestic, strong, and firmly established. Reach out to Him as He is the rock of your salvation. Though it may seem everybody around you has let you down, you can depend on His love. Don't focus on the threats around you. Rather, focus on the throne above you! Let your testimony be Habakkuk 3:18-19:

"Yet I will rejoice in the LORD, I will be joyful in God my Savior. The Sovereign LORD is my strength; he makes my feet like the feet of a deer, he enables me to tread on the heights of mountains."

<u>How to Overcome Life's Difficulties</u>

- Prevail in Prayer.

- Pursue the Promises.

- Persist in Patience.

- Proclaim His Praise.

- Promote His Purpose.

13

Letting God Cultivate Your Life

"Plant the good seeds of righteousness, and you will harvest a crop of love. Plow up the hard ground of your hearts, for now is the time to seek the Lord, that He may come and shower righteousness upon you"
(Hosea 10:12).

During planting season in the rural farming community in which I live, plowing and fertilizing are faithfully done with the hopeful expectation there will be a great harvest. All the elements of successful agricultural planning don't happen automatically. There's a marked intelligence that is brought to bear by the farmer in the choosing of machinery, the selection of certain seed for certain soil, the grafting of plants and trees, all of which gives way to peas, potatoes, corn, peanuts, cotton, and fruit of all kinds.

But there is another kind of gardening, a higher form of culture, going on all the while in the minds and hearts of every one of us. What kind of cultivation are we giving to the spiritual possibilities of our souls? This should be a question of great interest for every individual and family, not just the church. The Bible says,

"You are God's field" (1 Corinthians 3:9).

If we will submit to Him in loving obedience He will superintend the culture of our spiritual life and will bring forth as a result something far more beautiful and splendid than we could ever hope for.

Hosea 14:5-7 says,

"I (God) will be to Israel like a refreshing dew from Heaven; my people will blossom like the lily; it will send roots deep into the soil like the cedars of Lebanon. Its branches will spread out like beautiful olive trees as fragrant as the cedar of Lebanon. My people will again live under my shade. They will flourish like grain and blossom like grapevines."

The dew comes as a welcomed relief during the dry season. God doesn't forget those who trust Him in times of drought. His dew will keep the branches from withering and fainting during the summer.

A characteristic of Christian character is that of growth, always seeking the next stage of maturity. The Bible says, "My people will grow as the lily". The lily grows rapidly and blooms in fragrance, so those who trust God will have abundant growth.

Another characteristic of the faithful Christian is someone who's well-rooted in their convictions and confidence. "Their roots will be deep in the soil like the cedars of Lebanon." Lebanon possessed great cedar forests in Biblical times. These tall trees had great roots to run deep underground and hold the tree secure in times of storm. The roots serve yet another purpose. Running far below the surface of the soil, they act as pumps to tap the hidden streams of water, giving the tree life during the long summer time. A Christian's roots of faith run down deep into the soil of God's promises. They tap streams of communion with God through prayer and fellowship with Christ.

When all earthly promises fail, the Christian's hope is not destroyed, because of the comfort that is drawn from the hidden confidence in God. When the winds of opposition blow hardest, the soul stands in strong assurance that God can keep His children and bring them to victory.

"Its branches will spread out like beautiful olive trees, as fragrant as the cedars of Lebanon"— I can remember, as a little boy and later as a teen, wandering around in my grandparent's backyard. They had four or five huge cedar trees with wide branches growing along the fence line. Not only did they provide wonderful shade in the summertime, there was a distinct, refreshing smell that only an evergreen could produce. The smell was almost intoxicating, and I often revisit those days in my mind.

The Scripture from Hosea 14 offers a picture as we

ought to be as Christians. In the heart of God there's a cherished ideal of us that is beautiful and fragrant like that. We must realize it! And live it out as if we belong to it, because we do! The world needs for its tired and wretched eyes the beauty of Christian character. The world needs to be refreshed by the fragrance of unselfish deeds and Christian conduct.

This kind of life isn't only good for the one in whom it characterizes, it's beneficial to those who are about to faint and are ready to die. These poor souls come under the restful shade of such character and can be revived with hope. What a blessed thing it is to live in such fellowship with God that the simplicity of Christ's spirit in us can cheer the faint, inspire the discouraged, and bring comfort to those that mourn. Stand tall as the cedar and shower those around you with the fragrance of true love, God's love.

14

Building a House of Character

"We can rejoice when we run into problems and trials, for we know that they help us develop endurance. And endurance develops strength of character, and character strengthens our confident hope of salvation. And this hope will not lead to disappointment"
(Romans 5:3-5).

I once told the congregation of a small country church that I pastored, "We are all in the construction business. Not only are we building the Kingdom of God through the ministries of our church, we are building something else personally significant to each one of us. Our thoughts, emotions, words, and actions are always in a state of work, building a house not made with hands, but built with the imperishable fabric of our souls".

The most important house you can build is your character. It is better to live in one small room where the soul dwells with integrity and righteousness and the window lets in the realm of spiritual beauty, than to live in the biggest city, in the tallest building, on the most fashionable street, where the soul dwells in a dark cellar devoid of light or hope.

We are all building our own house. In this modern world, if a person has enough wealth, they can hire a builder to construct a house based on a certain plan and then go their own way. They do not have to be troubled by it until the house is finished. But a person cannot build character by proxy. It's a personal endeavor that must be built day by day, year by year by the personal strokes of our own hammer. It's continuous and a person must spend a lifetime building it.

A person cannot build good character, then go off and do what they please and come home to find it just the same as they left it. Some people think this way. There are some people who think because they were converted twenty, thirty, forty years ago, and built-up a degree of religious experience, there's nothing else needed to be improved or maintained. There could be no greater mistake than this. The house of character is in a constant state of building and can never be left to take care of itself. Until the day we die we must be builders. Matthew 24:6-13 says,

"You will hear of wars, but don't panic, nations will go to war against other nations, you will be persecuted because you're my followers, many will turn away from me, false

prophets will appear, many people's love will grow cold, but the one who endures to the end will be saved."

The blessings of God come all the time. But there's no blessedness so sacred that it allows the Christian to stop building personal character. Just because a child grows up, leaves the home, and no longer is within hearing distance of their parent's voice, doesn't mean he has all the knowledge he needs to survive. It's one of the pervading principles that the more delicate a thing is, the sooner it will decay and fall to pieces when it's separated from the root in which it sprang. Consider the flower, nature's perfume will eventually evaporate from it, and the petals will fall off soon after it has left the stalk.

Many people don't exercise their faith, some choose to ignore it and they wonder why the joy of living has jumped the fence and gone loose. Good things, like character, must be improved upon, maintained, and built up if they're to enjoy the abundant life Christ wants us all to enjoy.

If we did good work yesterday, it's easier to do good work today. This makes it easier for work to be done tomorrow. Because a house is beautiful yesterday, doesn't prevent us from improving it in future days. It's true that life is what we make it. Everyone who comes to know Christ's divine message, will build a house of conduct and character. And each house will be tested. The wind will blow on it, the rain will beat against it. No house, no matter how well it's constructed, will escape a thorough testing in every part. There's no basis whatsoever in the Bible for the delusional dream that it's possible for a Christian to reach an ecstatic holiness beyond the danger of temptation. Every character illustration God has given us in the Bible, who has sought to build up character pleasing to Him, speaks to us in their testimony of the universal struggle and battle with the storms of life. Be assured, your house of character will be tried by the wind and drenched by the rain.

The temptations that are initiated by the devil are a flagrant attempt to assault your body, mind, and soul. They will sweep over you and are as real and as terrible as at any time in the history of the world. Because of this, there's a requirement that everyone's house of character have a solid foundation on which they can build character that will stand through all the storms of temptation that beat down on it. Jesus said,

"Anyone who listens to my teaching and follows it is wise, like a person who builds a house on solid rock. Though the rain comes in torrents and the flood waters rise and the winds beat against that house, it won't collapse because it's built on bedrock" (Matthew 7:24-25).

It's clear that the rock which Jesus sets forth as a safe foundation for our house of human life is that of obedience to him. He has promised to take care of those who in obedient humility do his will.

81

15

Use What God Gives You

"God has given each of you a gift from his great variety of spiritual gifts. Use them well to serve one another. Do it with all the strength and energy that God supplies. Then everything you do will bring glory to God through Jesus Christ. All glory and power to him forever and ever!"
(1 Peter 4:10-11)

When my son graduated from high school, he wasted no time in pursuing career opportunities. His part time job in real estate motivated him to study, complete, and pass the initial real estate license exam. He also enrolled full-time in college. Although the future is bright for him in the business world, he's still cognizant that his life is worth more than a vocation. We've talked about divine purpose and divine providence. And the ultimate use of our God-given abilities. It does a person a great deal of good to see the potential in life and know that life presents many opportunities if we look for them.

Sometimes at superficial glance there seems to be a

great waste in human life. I read the following story as told by a preacher long ago. He said he had the good fortune of being invited to stay with a family in their beautiful farmhouse in the country. The woman of the house met him with a smile, but he sensed sorrow in her voice. After a little conversation, she showed him to his room.

As she opened the door, she lowered her voice and said, "I'm going to give you the room that was my daughters who is now in heaven. Everything in it is just as it was when she left it. The books on the shelves, pictures hanging on the wall, the vases and photographs on the mantel and the furniture in the room are just the same as when she went away."

She stepped across the room to a beautiful old-fashioned bookcase and pointed to a rolled parchment tied with a pretty pink ribbon, "And there's her diploma, lying just as she threw it there when she came home from college, and only a few days before she got sick. I came up with her to the room, and she flung the diploma in there and it stuck at an angle just like you see it. My daughter closed the door on it and said she was glad she got it. It hasn't been touched since. Two weeks later, I buried her beside her father. But there lies her unused diploma that cost her so much hard work, and that she was so proud to obtain."

This sweet mother had the painful feeling there had

somehow been a great waste in all the hard work her daughter had performed to earn her diploma. In her mind, the diploma represented an education that her daughter was not permitted to use on earth. This story, though unique in its circumstance, seems to happen to young and old all the time. People are always acquiring knowledge, learning trades, and disciplines which they never seem to have the opportunity of using. Many people hesitate to pay the price in sacrifice and hard work to enlarge their scope of wisdom, for fear they'll never have any opportunity to get a valuable return for it in dollars and cents. The internal debate for many young people on their way to college is the question, "Will this pay off for me?" After performing a great miracle, Jesus told his disciples,

"Now, gather the leftovers, so that nothing is wasted" (John 6:12).

The most important thing about getting an education isn't whether it will make the young person wealthy; the great question is will it make them a person of character? Will it make them noble and responsible? Will it give them an imaginative mind? Will they use it to help others and not just themselves? So many people enter the professional world like a mass of struggling ants climbing up an exaggerated ant-hill trying to get to the top first. Goals and aspirations are to be admired, but is there a vision of God's greater purpose for the person who achieves? The world looks out for self. We must realize there's a mighty battle going on, and that every human heart has joy and sorrow. Nothing of another person's concern should be seen as wasteful or commonplace.

It seems to me that today we need "all-around" young men and women. Whatever calling or profession a person chooses, we need to promote the healthy idea that you should be more than a doctor, lawyer, preacher, teacher, construction worker, farmer, architect, lineman, clerk, accountant, cook, business owner, engineer, janitor, police officer, or housekeeper. Be first, a well-rounded, well-informed man, woman, or child with character. The more generous you are in your education of mind and heart, the greater your personality will be, not only in your chosen line of business, but in the larger relation you have with the world.

No honest work which we do to enlarge our scope of knowledge and clarify our mental and spiritual vision is ever wasted. We need this ability so that the mountains, the beaches, the woodlands, gardens and fields, and the hearts of people we meet reveal the goodness and glory of God. This is never a waste. The unused diplomas of life help us practice for the greater world of heaven in which Christians will enjoy. Honesty on earth will be honesty in heaven. Patience on earth will be patience in heaven. On earth, the faith, hope, and love we use to achieve, will be celebrated and practiced in heaven. The eternal strides we make on earth are the ones that lead us to heaven.

Let us go on gathering all the knowledge we can and cultivate it into our hearts and minds. What appears to be an unused diploma or insignificant occurrence is never wasted. God used a little boy's five loaves of bread and two fish to feed thousands (John 6:1-14). Even the left-over fragments were useful! Do you have questions about your future?

> ***"Seek the Kingdom of God above all else, and live righteous-***
> ***ly, and He will give you everything you need"***
> ***(Matthew 6:33).***

Be all you can be and use every experience while seeking out what God has in store for you.

16

Calm Arguments by Preventing the Fire

*"Remind everyone about these things, and command them in
God's presence to stop fighting over words. Such
arguments are useless, and they can ruin those who
hear them"*
2 Timothy 2:14.

How many times have you been guilty of causing a negative situation to get worse by talking when silence would've been the best decision? Ever since the 1940s, the United States Forest Service has used "Smokey the Bear" to teach people to be responsible with camp fires. Considering this analogy, we can relate this lesson to a verse found in the Book of Proverbs:

"Fire goes out without wood, and quarrels disappear when gossip stops. A quarrelsome person starts fights as easily as hot embers light charcoal or fire lights wood"

(Proverbs 26:20).

This important lesson is for all of us. And it should

encourage us to recognize that if we refuse to engage in gossip, bitterness, or hold to judgmental attitudes; it puts out the fire of argument in other people's lives.

A famous author once said, "I learned long ago, never to wrestle with a pig. You get dirty, and besides, the pig likes it." It is hard to resist the temptation to talk about someone who's wronged you, especially a person who tries to discredit you or drag you down. There's no convincing an individual who's purposefully looking for an excuse to start a fire.

Sadly, judging others is our favorite pastime. Judging makes us feel good because it puts us in a better light than others. Regardless of which side you are on or who may be at fault, the more mature individual will focus on what lies ahead rather than to dwell in the past. In spiritual matters you may be prone to being pulled down in despair when you recall past sins; especially when someone tries to remind you and others of your faults. As the "Accuser", Satan attempts to makes us feel that our sins are too great to ever be forgiven or forgotten.

We are never more like God than when we chose to forgive. It is no one's rightful place to judge another person. We are all sinners, but because of Christ, we're loved by God. A person's salvation is never contingent upon their personal perfection; although some people act like it. Salvation is never something we earn; God loves us all just because He chose to love us, which is why Christ paid the ultimate price on the Cross so that we could be saved.

Rendering judgement upon someone for their past sins isn't a responsibility of yours, the pastor, or anyone else; that's solely God's job. Matthew 7:1-3 says,

"Don't judge others, and you will not be judged. For you will be treated as you treat others. The standard you use in judging is the standard by which you will be judged. And why worry about a speck in your friend's eye when you have a log in your own?"

When we hold grudges, gossip, and refuse to forgive, we are not allowing God to control us, but choosing to hold to our selfish ways.

A Christian's job is not to judge one another. A Christian's job is to share Christ and pray for others. Don't let someone, because of their judgmental ways, convince you you're not worthy of great things and of use in His Kingdom. God can do great things with us regardless of our past. The greatest gift we can offer others is the Good News that God looks beyond our past to give us grace for the future.

Mistakes are what make the gospel such Good News! God can and will redeem you from everything, EVERY-THING! Remember this: There are two ways a fire can die. You can pour water on the flames or starve the fire of oxygen. Sometimes you must apologize for things you didn't do in order to help people move on. Other times, when you've done all you can do, you must ignore the continued comments of people who oppose you and allow your actions to speak for themselves.

Situations will call for different approaches but be ready to resist the urge to retaliate or respond to an unjust criticism; instead, calm your heart, clear your head, and act in accordance with the love and understanding you would want for yourself. You can solve many problems by refusing to add fuel to an already unwise fire. We can all prevent forest fires!

17

A Light Heart Helps Carry a Heavy Burden

"Share each other's burdens, and in this way obey
the law of Christ"
(Galatians 6:2).

There are many remedies offered for the ills of life. As a chaplain I'm often sought after to help people gain relief from the stresses in their life. But I don't always have an immediate cure for them. Many of these folks have either become overwhelmed to the point they can't see beyond a great mountain in front of them or they haven't ever considered the Higher Power in relation to their problems.

At one of my battle assemblies where I was serving as an Army chaplain, a Soldier within my unit came rushing up to me as soon as our initial formation was over, "Chaplain, I'm sure glad to see you! I need to talk because I don't know what I'm going to do about my situation!" He seemed desperate and I could tell by the look in his eyes that his heart was heavy. This soldier is not the only one who has ever had a heavy heart. In fact, the world is full of heavy-hearted people. All of us must fight life's battles and it's not easy. There are no avoiding difficulties completely, they come to the rich and the poor. No amount of possessions (cars, trucks, or boats) have the power to take us away from all that burden our hearts. And because problems and troubles come to all, there must be a universal solution; something that's within the reach of every person. What is it that can help all of us to lighten the load on our heart and affections? Victory over our problems begins by being equipped for the battle.

The first secret to a light heart is friendship. The one thing that can keep us from falling into despair is the conscious idea that we have a good, strong, faithful friend to which we can turn. It's a great mistake to live in this world without cultivating friends. It's a relief to us to encounter a sympathetic touch from a kindred spirit. Friendships are made even greater when centered on the spirit of Christ. Jesus said, to his disciples, and through them to us:

"You are my friends" (John 15:15).

Friendship is part of the formula in attaining a light heart.

Another secret to a light heart is appreciation by others. Having the consciousness that we know of someone who thinks well of us, has a positive effect on us mentally and emotionally. Being appreciated carries with it the responsibility of returning that good will. Knowing someone cares and admires you promotes a glad heart and helps us face the day with music in our soul. Think of this, if we live honestly toward God, trying to please Him in everything, we can know we have His favor. Is it not true that much of the unrest within our heart comes from the feeling that others are not pleased with us? There's only one way to lighten your heart of that feeling, and that's to "set the record straight".

Many people who talk to me about conflict in their relationships have either wronged someone or they have been wronged themselves. All joy and peace are gone, their heads are lowered or turned away, and their heart is heavy. When apologies and confessions are exchanged and the wrong-doer's been forgiven, faces brighten, and hearts are lighter. When we trespass God's law, and the Holy Spirit sweeps in with loving, but firm conviction, our hearts become heavy. The way to lighten our heart and become happy again is to frankly confess our sins and receive forgiveness.

Another secret of a light heart is the conscious effort we put forth to be helpful. The person who is most waited on or petted is often the one that is so far down emotionally they've lost their sense of helping others. Selfishness clips our wings and we will fail to move beyond ourselves. Selfishness is like a bowl of heavy dough that doesn't rise but sinks where it is and becomes soggy and sour. Fill your heart with a selfish attitude and you'll never know the joy that helps you overcome your own hardships. The consciousness that we're helping somebody, making them happier, will bring a ray of sunshine home to us and make life a little more bearable.

Finally, a light heart is possible when we have the assurance that this is God's world and not the devils. Though we can't see how any good will come of it, God is orchestrating a symphony that will play a melody that's tuned to our own ears. There's a bright side to any difficulty and God in His way and time makes us know that all things are working together for our good (Romans 8:28).

A beautiful passage from Psalm 61 speaks so clearly the feelings in many of our hearts:

"O God listen to my cry! Hear my prayer! From the ends of the earth, I cry to you for help when my heart is overwhelmed. Lead me to the towering rock of safety, for you are my safe refuge; safe beneath the shelter of your wings!" (Psalm 61:1-4).

Make note of these four secrets for a light heart and remember them when you need a cure for a heavy one: friendship, appreciation, consciousness of being helpful, and God's guidance. One of these can help you where you are right now in this moment, but all four are within your reach. I know so, because as a child of God, there are doors set before you just waiting to be walked through and only you can shut them. Be watchful and walk where God leads.

<u>The Cure for a Heavy Heart</u>

- Friendship.

- Appreciation by others.

- Conscious effort to help others.

- Assurance of God's guidance.

18

You are Only as Good as the Seeds You Sow

"Don't be misled. You will always harvest what you plant. Those who live only to satisfy their own sinful nature will harvest decay and death from that nature. But those who live to please the Spirit will harvest everlasting life from the Spirit"
(Galatians 6:7-8).

National Farmer's Day is celebrated in the month of October and there are very few people in North Santa Rosa County (Florida) that does not have a connection to a family that works the land in some way. Most folks in rural areas appreciate the hard labor it requires to produce crops. The farmer has a unique and challenging task; for its dependent on Mother Nature's sunshine and rain. Both of which are out of our control. Productive farming requires calculations and timing when it comes to planting seed and knowing when the crop is at its peak for harvest.

Agricultural references are a common theme throughout the Bible. The parable of the sower presents a powerful lesson pertaining to sowing and reaping, planting, and harvesting (Matthew 13:1-23). In another parable, Jesus portrays the human mind and heart as fields where rival farmers are competing for an opportunity to sow their seed and win the harvest. In Matthew 13:24-30, Jesus plants the good seed and afterward the devil comes as an enemy and plants tares in the field. When this happens, in many cases the loving purpose of Christ is defeated in our lives, because the harvest yields bundles of tares only fit to be burned.

In still another passage, the Bible talks about seed being planted in our heart and how God makes them grow. Somebody plants it and another waters it; they work together for the same purpose. And both will be rewarded for their hard work.

"We are God's field" (1 Corinthians 3:6-9).

All these passages present principles in which we can gain wisdom and develop the mind of Christ to which daily life can be enhanced. The prophet Hosea writes,

"Plant the good seeds of righteousness, and you will harvest a crop of love. Plow up the hard ground of your hearts, for now is the time to seek the Lord, that He may come and shower righteousness on you" (Hosea 10:12).

This single verse is not addressed to those who don't

know God, but to those who have trusted God, but for some reason have   neglected their spiritual nature. This lack of watchfulness causes a heart to become hardened and unproductive.

Anyone that's spent any amount of time working on a farm knows what fallow ground means. The soil was once in cultivation and yielded crops, but due to indolence or crop rotation, the farmer has let the plows stand idle in that piece of land. In this case, the ground becomes packed and hard. Weeds and grass often take up residence on fallow ground. Such a field must be worked to prepare it for future harvests. The prophet Hosea says those who have become cold and indifferent in their relations to God are in that condition, and he calls upon all such people to break up the fallow ground.

So how does that happen? How can we plow up the fallow ground of our hearts? The first and greatest of all spiritual cultivation is prayer. I don't mean a single out-pouring of petition to God because of some impulse or personal emergency for shelter and protection. God hears these prayers. But I'm referring to the great urge for pur-poseful, regular prayer at a stated time because you know that the Holy Spirit, who carries the Wisdom of God, is waiting for you to receive it. This kind of prayer is based on a yearning for divine communion with the mightiest force known to human kind. It's a marvel of God that He hears and answers all your prayers. In my opinion, there's no such thing as unanswered prayers; it's either "yes, no, or wait." For thorough spiritual cultivation, prayer must be a priority for the one who wants answers and understanding. It's a duty and privilege for God's children to keep their hearts worshipful, reverent, and in a proper state of cultivation to receive every good seed the Divine Farmer (God) seeks to plant in their soul. To do so is to be in a proper condition to bring a rapid, thorough, and mature harvest that graces the Spirit of God.

I am compelled to share that prayer meetings are often less attended by church members and that's a concern to me. The habit of stated prayer at regular times for the Christian church is to some extent falling into neglect. And I am sure that no Christian can live as they ought to live, exercising the influence they should and yield glory to God, without consciously devoting certain time every day to sincere worship of God. Prayer develops a spiritual atmosphere wherever it's practiced. There's a heightened spiritual awareness that takes place in the mind and heart of the one that prays. This makes it easier for the spiritual life to grow and thrive.

There are some people who have intellectual conceptions concerning spiritual things and who claim to be Christian in theory. But the condition of their heart, if not totally surrendered to God, is not entirely Christian. It's the divine influence of prayer that creates within a person Christian truths that flourish and grow. A wise farmer works the land to glean what is produced. And a wise person will cultivate the "soil" of the heart to receive God's planted seed. A wise farmer plows the fields at regular times without reference to the amount of corn that it will yield. A wise person will ready their heart so the seeds will grow under the right conditions. A wise farmer turns the soil over and over, to keep it in a proper state of cultivation in which to grow a certain crop. A wise person takes the sensitive fields of the heart and consciously opens it to God; communing with Him concerning all the deep longings and aspirations that are our highest nature and greatest concern.

19

The Royal Standard of Joy

"Don't be dejected and sad, for the joy of the Lord is your strength!"
(Nehemiah 8:10).

A group of tourists were visiting the British capital while the changing of the guard was taking place at Buckingham Palace. A British man remarked, "I don't see the Royal Standard flying today."

"Royal Standard, what does that mean?" inquired one of the tourists.

"Don't you know lad?" was the surprised answer. "The flag shows if the Majesty is in residence!"

Joy is like that. True joy in the heart is the flag which announces that the King of Kings has taken residence in the hearts and lives of a Christian. Jesus himself will banish all gloom and despair from our lives due to his abiding presence in each of us.

Problems and pain are everywhere. But that's not the

completed story for anyone who trusts in God. For the Christian, problems and pain, while real and serious, are ultimately incidental. The truest of all facts is that God loves you and me and our biggest problem, sin, has been dealt with and accounted for through the Cross of Christ. So, there's reason to rejoice no matter what. Philippians 4:4 tells us,

"Always be full of joy in the Lord. I say it again, rejoice!"

It can be incredibly hard at times to parade joy in our outward expressions. In the course of your day and the duties you perform, there come experiences that will leave you far from joyful. God understands why we struggle with 24/7 positivity. Truthfully, there are many times when we feel the stronger urge to complain instead. God understands this. The psalms are full of these expressions. But you and I can guard against a joyless life by working the formulas Jesus Christ gives to us:

"Ask, using my name and you will receive, and you will have abundant joy" (John 16:24).

All the joy you can possibly need is available for the asking. There's no need to drag through another gloomy day.

Sometimes amid the inevitable busy lifestyles we lead, we may forfeit the joy God intends for us to experience and to share. A Christian once said, "When I met Christ, I felt that I had swallowed sunshine!" We must hang on to life with a tenacious faith that says God is good no matter what things look like on the outside. God is faithful, good, trustworthy, loyal, and loving. The time to rejoice in God is always now! Even on life's most difficult days, you may rest assured that God is in Heaven and He still cares.

The way faith works is that we don't feel our way into action. But because of what we believe and know to be true, we act. Your belief should dictate your actions. So, if you believe Jesus when he said, "I have told you these things so that you'll be filled with my joy. Yes, your joy will overflow!"—you know you're capable of rejoicing in God. It takes practice and a complete giving over to the mind of Christ to recite who God is and what He's done for you. Let nothing stop you. Think about what He's planned for you. God's plan includes blessings of joy, but you must believe His promises and claim them as your own. Only in God can true happiness and contentment be found. Your joyful spirit can serve as a powerful example to your friends and family. Not everything in your life is how you would like it to be. The Bible says:

"A bad attitude or broken spirit drains a person's strength,
but a joyful heart is good medicine
(Proverbs 17:22).

So, rejoice anyway and your mind and spirit will work in tandem.

The key to joy is your prayer life. Prayer will keep the "Royal Standard" flying. It'll make you a joyous Christian and joy is contagious. It spills over to bless your family, church, and friends. Eventually, it will make people ask you, "What keeps you so cheerful all the time?" Cultivate your spiritual experiences with God so that you'll be able to share why you have hope and joy. In this way, you'll help them be stronger to effectively meet their own life challenges.

20

Overcoming Life's Battles Through Praise

"Praise the Lord, you armies of angels who serve Him and do His will! Praise the Lord, everything He has created, everything in all His Kingdom. Let all that I am praise the Lord" (Psalm 103:21-22).

I have discovered perhaps like many of you that singing songs in your car while driving can help you cope with daily stresses. There's a certain release that comes with it. A song of praise can sink into your soul. And through a posture of worship, you can be made free from the shackles of worldly attacks and bombardment of issues. You can know that no matter what happens or what you must face, the Lord is with you and you have a present help, always. That's what praise during a battle can do for you!

In seasons of our lives it can feel like we're fighting one battle after another. It's important to know we can win these wars by following a divine strategy the great warrior, King David followed:

"The Lord is my light and my salvation. So, why should I be afraid? The Lord is my fortress, protecting me from danger, so why should I tremble? When evil comes to devour me, when my enemies and foes attack me, they will stumble and fall. Though a mighty army surrounds me, my heart will not be afraid. Even if I am attacked, I will remain confident" (Psalm 27:1-3).

In this passage, while the words indicate hope and confidence, the central theme is about a battle. While it may seem to be imaginary, many of our battles in life feel overwhelming and we feel like we're being attacked. David writes that his enemies are coming after him, but he's not afraid. Armies are deploying against him, but he's confident. War is breaking out, but his enemies fall. Whether David is using this as a metaphor to describe life or perhaps an actual war is going on around him, he finds himself on the defensive. During it all, he knows the One who will give him shelter.

We all go through seasons where life feels like a battle. Communication in your relationships feel like a warzone; situations at work feel like everyone has allied themselves against you. You receive a bad health report and it seems like the enemy dropped a bomb on you; someone takes advantage of your kind nature, manipulates you, and talks behind your back. In these difficult situations and in many others like them, when life feels like a battle, how do you stay confident and hopeful? Where can you go for strength and safety?

While serving on a military mission in a very austere environment, it seemed as if Mother Nature had it out for the Soldiers of our collective units. It was a challenge conducting maneuvers and convoys under the desert sun in 110-degree temperatures. We were tired, on-edge, double-tasked, missing family members back home, and having to tactfully be on guard for simulated assaults from the enemy. Commanders expect their Soldiers to perform despite the conditions. The United States has the best trained military in the world. But our troops are not machines, they are human beings who have a soul that need strength to endure the spiritual battles they face. We're all soldiers of God fighting in this army.

Using King David's example, we can profit by praising God because of the following reasons:

Praise activates faith. When fighting a battle praising the Lord may require a step of faith. You may not feel like praising the Lord, but to do so generates and activates faith. Praising God overrides doubts and says, "I believe God, anyhow!" An element that is critical to spiritual warfare is that praising God breaks down Satan's defenses.

Praise stimulates hope. When a person enters a season of praise to our Heavenly Father it automatically and necessarily brings one to hope in God. Hope follows praise. Psalm 42:5 says,

"I will put my hope in God, and once again I will praise Him, my Savior and my God."

Praising the Almighty is a positive step, an upward look, a declaration of faith. These things bring hope into focus. Jesus Christ, God's only Son, is the hope of the world. Money, power, and war cannot meet our eternal needs, but he can.

Praise increases love. Personal experience has shown me that it's almost impossible to praise the Lord and hold a grudge at the same time. Hostility and resentment and praise do not go together. When we praise the Lord, He becomes the object of our affection, thus increasing our love toward Him and others.

During chaotic circumstances, David gained strength through worshipping God. Worship helps pull us above our circumstances. It reminds us that when God is for us no one can be against us and win. In seasons when your life feels like a battle, win the war by praising God.

<u>Praising God Does These Things</u>

- Activates Faith.

- Stimulates Hope.

- Declares Faith.

- Increases Love.

21

True Loves Lives in the Heart

"Where your treasure is, there the desires of your heart will also be"
(Matthew 6:21).

Many clear heads have gone to ruin through the power of a bad heart; and many weak heads have worn a crown of glory because of the strength of a good heart. The world will pass away, and all its glory will fade as a leaf, but the heart lives on.

Originally sculptured in Rome are the "Four Seasons Statutes". Spring is a delicate girl with flowers in her long hair. She has a hopeful look upon her face. Summer is a woman with full lips, face, and figure. She looks healthy and vibrant. Heads of wheat are in her hair and she has a satisfied look on her face. Autumn is the same face, just a little older with a crown of clustered grapes. She looks back ever so slightly as if in retrospect. Winter has a rigid, gaunt face with pine cones intertwined in her hair.

The marble statutes speak not only of earth's seasons, but also of the rapid progression of human life. All life's promises on earth end in decay except when the heart is kept sweet and young by having fellowship with Jesus. Our youthful outlook is also buoyed by the hope of eternal life. The Bible sets forth many references concerning the heart. Solomon says in Proverbs 23:26,

"Oh, my son, give me your heart. May your eyes take delight in following my ways."

Meaning, that if the heart is given then it will be a complete and prosperous surrender. Proverbs 4:23 instructs us:

"Guard your heart above all else, for it determines the course of your life."

Anselm of Canterbury says that our heart is like a mill which a certain man told his servant to grind only the best grain, whether it be wheat, barley, or oats. He told him he would make his living this way. But there was a certain other man who was jealous and sought to discredit the servant's reputation for producing good meal. He would sneak around and anytime he found the mill unattended he would throw gravel in it to clog it or mix dirt and chaff with the meal. If the servant was faithful in watching, he produced beautiful flour which was a delight to his master. But if he did not and the enemy tampered with the mill, the master would become angry and not pay his servant. Our hearts are like the mill. They're ever grinding on the thoughts and imaginations in which we feed them. The devil is our enemy and he seeks to discredit us by throwing in evil thoughts. The darkness is prevented by watchfulness and prayer. Jesus Christ says,

"A good person produces good things from the treasury of a good heart, and an evil person produces evil things from the treasury of an evil heart" (Matthew 12:35).

When a person lives daily in a spirit of prayer and feels the touch of God's love, eternal youth will characterize the faithful heart. It's no wonder Christ asks for our heart; for nobody cares for a thing unless it comes from the heart. When a person gives you a sincere compliment or tells you, "I love you with all my heart", we value their words even more because it originates from the purest and most important part of their being.

A little girl with a handful of violets once knocked on the door of a preacher's house. His wife answered, "How may I help you?"

"I have this offering of flowers from my mother," replied the little girl.

"Your mother, child? Didn't she die last autumn?"

"That's true, ma'am," said the girl, "And your husband prayed at her grave and said my mother's soul in all of its fullness would blossom in heaven. These are the first violets which have bloomed on my mother's grave. I have plucked them, and I like to think she sends them to you with greetings from her heart. And mine too."

The preacher overheard the little girl's sweet words and his eyes moistened. As he took the flowers from her tender hand, he put them in the outer pocket of his coat and said, "This is a gift from the heart, given out of true love."

Revelations 3:20 quotes Jesus,

"Look! I stand at the door and knock. If you hear my voice and open the door, I will come in and be your friend."

So, Jesus Christ says he is knocking at the door of your heart. If you let him come in, he will stay with you as a sacred guest, forever—a beacon of hope, a symbol of peace, and a love like you've never known.

22

Nature Can Recharge the Soul

"Jesus took some apostles into the woods to be alone and one of them said, it's wonderful for us to be here!"
(Matthew 17:1,4).

After a productive day at work I find myself looking forward to entering the sanctuary of the great outdoors. Trail running has turned into the one thing that gives me a much needed physical, mental, and spiritual uplift. For me, time spent running between trees, along creeks, by green shrubs, and on dirt roads does something to heighten my spiritual perspective. I must confess part of my woodland love is most likely an inherited trait from my parents and grandparents, for both sets were raised in the country and did not lack for good wholesome outdoor activity. Growing up in a rural community helped me appreciate the words of John Denver's hit song, "Take Me Home Country Roads", because that's how I was raised.

Growing up country was full of wonderful memories for me. And I can't think of heaven without something of the freedom that being in the outdoors brings. The forest and the woodland landscape of the country are full of healing because there the trees grow to their fullness and perfection. There's blessedness in that and I like to be among the beauty of it. There is color, vibrancy, and life to be enjoyed in the woods. To forsake its invitation is to take part of living for granted.

During my trail runs mockingbirds, cardinals, wrens, and warblers line the road ways. Crows can often be heard holding their conventions with their calls being loud and proud. The blue jays play their pranks among the brush. The yellowhammer and woodpeckers do their carpentry and exploit the wood of an aging tree. The quail scamper across the road in front of me and the foxes lay in wait hoping to outwit a rodent for a nice afternoon meal.

Running deep into the woods, there's a growing fragrance near the place where the creek runs along the trail. This is where the spring seeps from the ground and rare delicate ferns grow along the sides. Green moss covers the rocks that line the edge of the creek bed and they serve as a carpet leading the wild animals to the water source.

The continuous evergreen fragrance of the pine and the

cedar trees elicit a sense of healing. I like to think this evergreen aroma is a perfume of God's own medicine for tired men and weary women.

The woods are full of precious things of every sort. Jonathan, of the Bible, David's best friend, once found a bee tree in the woods and he filled himself with the sweet honey. The Bible says,

"Now all the people of the land came to a forest; and when the people had come into the woods, there was honey, dripping. Jonathan stretched out the end of the rod that was in his hand and dipped it in a honeycomb and put his hand to his mouth; and his countenance was brightened, and he felt refreshed" (1 Samuel 14:25-27).

The woods are full of berries--edible ones; blackberries, their cousins the dew berry, blue berries, and even mulberries. I've often seen bullaces and scuppernongs hang from the vines of the trees right before the fall season. It's quite the thrill to shake the vines from the tallest trees and have the freshest and juiciest of all scuppernongs fall at your feet. It's like nature's candy falling all around you. Do you sense the purity of it? The woods have a healing nature and I call it my "hiding place".

Another secret of the woodlands is vast oceans become what they are because somewhere in the woods a small little brook is formed. Nothing is hardly sweeter than the evolution of a little brook; which feeds a creek, which feeds a small lake and eventually a river, which leads to the bay, then the gulf and the ocean.

Once while running on part of my favorite trail, a small, wild fawn rose up on its spindly legs. He trotted a few steps and stopped, and I stopped too. There was a mutual stare and then we both continued our way. I have run with cottontails, squirrels, and a myriad of other wild-life.

There's solace and lessons to be learned from the woods. Perhaps you need to get away and visit one near where you live. Maybe you too can have an experience with God in nature's solitude. The closer we get to God and the more we open our hearts to receive His rich bless-ings, not only will we be happier ourselves, but the more blessing and benefit we will be to all who are a part of our world. Like the psalmist David, we should all seek com-fort and our strength from a greater source; the Higher Power called God Almighty.

Whenever we find ourselves sick, weak, or in trouble there's the temptation to seek help from sources that are beneath God. We must not let that be our only source. Sickness, pain, and troubles of all kind can be rare bless-ings if it brings us into a closer fellowship with God. God is to be our lifeline and He can be found anywhere. But there is a significant beauty in feeling His presence in the woodlands with all its peacefulness.

23

Be Warm-Hearted, Not Snow Bound

*"Be kind to each other, tenderhearted, forgiving one another,
just as God through Christ has forgiven you"
(Ephesians 4:32).*

In the South around harvest time cotton is often described as the "the snow of the south". It's a beautiful scene to look out across half-mile rows and see acres and acres of beautiful white cotton scattered along the country side. The "real snow" that falls during the cold months in other parts of the country, can be equally delightful; that is unless there is lots of it and it hinders your travel.

Several years ago, when I was the head coach of a men's cross-country team, we traveled to North Carolina during the off-season for an indoor track meet. The forecast called for snow and the team, being from Florida, looked forward to the possibility of seeing snow accumulation. Some members of the team had never seen snow! The team spent the night at the YMCA Blue Ridge Assembly in Black Mountain and woke the next morning to 8 inches of freshly fallen snow. It was an alluring scene and the runners cared more about snowball fights than running fast times in their races. Besides having to help them refocus on the purpose of our trip, I had to cautiously consider driving on snow and ice-covered roads through the mountains. None of the roads were closed, but everyone knew we were driving at our own risks. There are many cuts in the narrow roads between Black Mountain and Boone, North Carolina, and when snow comes with wind drifts, these cuts fill, and it's slow-go for traveling. The snow was so deep in some parts, snow plows were getting stuck in steep ridges and inclines.

On another occasion when we were traveling to the same place for the same reason we spent an extra night because the snow had accumulated so much. On our way back home, we made it into north Georgia and found the traffic at a standstill. The interstate was packed, cars were sliding off the road, and people were turning their cars around in the median for lack of patience. Many of these impatient travelers were getting stuck in the slushy ice mixture. At one point the team decided to bail out of the van and play the role of Good Samaritan and help push cars out of the ruts. We were fortunate in not being detained longer than 2 hours. On some roads, during both trips, people were snow-bound for more than a day.

It is not only in the Blue Ridge Mountains that people get snow-bound. In an intellectual, moral, and spiritual way people may get snow-bound. It can happen in the big cities, small towns, as well as in the mountains. I've seen people whose hearts were so cold and whose manners were so stiff and unhappy that it was impossible for them to get along healthily with other people.

A church was searching for a new pastor and the committee asked its 90-year-old church member what her favorite kind of minister was, and she said, "I like one with the chill taken off." In other words, she wanted one that wasn't snow-bound. All other things being equal, the warm-hearted, frank, friendly, and sympathetic man or woman will have the greatest potential in any business or profession and will distance themselves from the poor soul who is "snow-bound" and frozen in by their own selfishness and sour demeanor.

People of all walks of life will lose out on life's most valuable treasures; faithful friends and kindred spirits, if they display a cold and snow-bound personality. Even people with less natural gifts than others, with their warm heart and sympathetic interest in everybody, have been able to draw throngs of loyal friends and confidants. Everyone ought to cultivate a positive interest in the welfare of others.

The most charismatic personality to ever be portrayed in terms of loving others for who they are and not what they do, was Jesus Christ. In one scene described in the Bible (John 6:1-11), people followed Christ out into the country where he had gone to have a little rest and a quite talk with his disciples. But he didn't draw himself up in his shell and freeze these poor people to fear because they had intruded on his quite time. Instead, according to the Apostle Matthew's account of the same story,

"He (Jesus) had compassion on them" (Matthew 14:14).

A little boy who happened to be in the crowd gave Jesus his bread and fish. Jesus multiplied them and made a great dinner for the hungry and tired people. This little boy willingly gave what he had to Christ and followed him as the pattern of his life in warm-hearted treatment of others. People like him will never fail in society, the marketplace, or the home place. They might make a mistake, but it won't be because of some snow-bound attitude. Warm your hearts, forgive others, and don't hold grudges. Love covers a multitude of sins and contributes to the solution of every known problem in life.

24

Christ Came to Take Away Our Sins

"Look! The Lamb of God who takes away the sin of the world!" (John 1:29).

I tend to dwell on the bright side of things or at least I try. But it cannot escape a person, even a positive thinker, that this world has more corruption than we would like to admit. It taints our thinking and cultivates an attitude of suspicion, doubt, and fear for the future. Here and there, deadly swamps and treacherous quicksand make men and women prone to sinking down in despair. It can all be traced back to a three-letter word we know as sin. Sin has covered the earth with wars, bullies, harassment, and cruelty.

Enter Jesus Christ over 2,000 years ago who dared to take on the sins of the world; then and now. He attacked sin at its very core. On a silent night, a holy night many years ago he caught the eye and ear of all who heard of him. And he aroused the hope of all humankind. In Matthew 1:20-21, the angel proclaims,

"Don't be afraid, for a child will be born and you are to call him Jesus, for he will save people from their sins."

Christ would be no Savior worth talking about if he could not save people from their sins. That's what Christ was born to do, and that's what he's doing all the time. We can face the New Year ahead because Christ delivers us from the penalty of our past sins.

A mother came to a pastor and told him how her son was wandering away from God and how the clutches of sin was ruining his soul and body. With her face wet with tears and her hands clinched together she said, "How gladly I would die for him if I could set him back the same pure and wholesome boy that he was ten years ago." But this mother's love, as strong as it was, had no power to pay the penalty of sin and make it possible for her son's sin to be pardoned.

But, "God so loved the world" that He gave Christ to die for us and redeem us. He was God's own Son. He had no sin of his own to account for. He came to stand in our place and offer himself as a sacrifice for us. Peter says,

"Christ suffered for our sins once for all-time. He never sinned, but he died for the just and the unjust, that he would bring us safely home to God" (1 Peter 3:18).

Christ suffered for us that he might save us from the

one great cause which makes us suffer. It's sin that has brought suffering into the world and every cruel, bitter heartache that the world has known has come from that one source. People try to make themselves happy while all the time carrying past sins with them. Jesus Christ is the Prince of Peace and the only one who can certainly give peace to every human heart. Through his death and suffering he has conquered the great source of our suffering and sorrow.

A company of men, who had taken part in a rebellion during the Civil War, were captured and sentenced to have every tenth man shot; to deter others from the same kind of uprising. Among these were a father and his son. They were told to form a straight line. The first man and every tenth man thereafter were marked for death. The father and son stood together, and as the son counted the men along the line he discovered his father was a doomed man. He realized what it would mean to have his family left without the head of their household; his mother would become a widow, and their old home stripped of its life and joy. He made his father change places with him, and before the father could respond, his son fell dead in his stead. He became his father's substitute. The father many years later still could not speak of his son without breaking down with a quivering voice and tear-wet eyes. The son took his doom and died in his place.

From the moment sin entered the world we all became doomed. Then Jesus was born, lived, and stepped in our place. He took the smiting and died on the cross for our sins. Of all the things to be happy about this Christmas season, this is the greatest news that could happen for us. For nothing is so important as the eternal state of our soul. Is there no love today that rises within your heart to return gratitude and loving confession to the Christ? He was born and died to redeem and save you from the guilt and punishment due for your sins?

Christ sacrificed to take on suffering, loneliness, insult, anguish, and even death to save you and me. Give him your love through open confession of gratitude and thanksgiving.

"Because of our faith, Christ has brought us into this place of undeserved privilege where we now stand, and we confidently and joyfully look forward to sharing God's glory. God showed His great love for us by sending Christ to live and die for us while we were still sinners. So now we can rejoice in our wonderful new relationship with God because our Lord Jesus Christ has made us friends with God"
(Romans 8:2, 8, 11).

At Christmas time, remember the star, the manger, the shepherds, and the Wise Men. And most of all, let's give Jesus his place in our hearts and our lives. Remember the reason for the season!

25

Beauty is More Than Skin Deep

"Cloth yourself instead with the beauty that comes from within, the unfading beauty of a gentle and quite spirit, which is so precious to God" (1 Peter 3:4).

I recently read a story about a young woman who was mesmerized by testimonies about faith healing. She was a noble, educated, and cultivated woman, but she was born with several birth marks that covered half of her face. They were so pronounced they could not possibly escape the attention of anyone. Every glance of every passerby went straight to her heart like an arrow. Thinking of the faith healing, she approached her Sunday School teacher and asked if she ought to seek to have her blemishes taken away.

"Do you think," she said, with trembling lips, "Do you think God would heal me of these spots and make them disappear?"

"My dear," replied her teacher, "That's a perfectly

natural and legitimate question, but it's just something I would not know. I know God can do anything, but I don't think there's anything wrong with asking Him that. Why don't you ask Him also to make you beautiful and radiant on the inside too?"

With thanks and a higher degree of comfort, she prayed, "Dear God, if possible, allow my birthmarks and blemishes to fade away so that they no longer plague me with funny looks from other people. Nevertheless, not as I will, but Your will be done. And please Lord, help improve my inner-beauty and character. In Jesus name, Amen."

She stayed in her position of prayer for a few moments and before she rose from her kneeling position, there came to her subconscious the sweet words from God's Spirit, "My grace is sufficient for you."

And so, it proved, in the days to follow, outwardly she appeared the same, and yet not the same. An inner light and a supernal love transfigured her. It was mysterious and fascinating. The loveliness of her soul, the charm and glory of her spirit, overtook the lack of outward beauty.

While working as a youth minister several years ago, it was suggested we host a "Youth Lock-In for Girls". We picked a date, made the plans, and during the event I had some of the parents lead small group discussions to discover what top things or issues were most important to the girls that attended. The results: 1) Relationship to God; 2) Loyal friendships; 3) Beauty and appearance. Many years later I wonder if the results would be the same for this generation. It's my belief these topics are still high on the list.

Many things that come from the strength and beauty of the body are from an environment of wealth and luxury. To some degree they are attained by working out or working for them. There have been women who have had strength and beauty but failed in the end of being loved. The real secret to loveliness lies beneath all that. It lies in the character and personality of the person. It's possible for every girl and woman to have charm which draws the sweetest gifts that can come to a person. There's a beauty of the soul and the spirit that can never die and will always attract love.

Allow me to share five Bible verses and a few words I recently read concerning girls, young ladies, and general womanhood:

1 Samuel 16:7 – "The Lord said, do not judge by a person's appearance or height. The Lord looks at the heart."

The world focuses on what people look like on the outside. God focuses on what people look like on the inside. Do you put more time and effort into being pretty on the outside or the inside? As a young girl grows older and becomes influenced by the world, there will be the temptation to spend more time trying to find the perfect outfit, get the perfect tan, find the perfect lip gloss, and have the perfect body. While there's nothing wrong with wanting to look attractive, there needs to be balance. The kind of girl who talks to God on a regular basis and reads her Bible develops her inner beauty.

Psalm 139:14 - "Thank you for making me so wonderfully complex! Your workmanship is marvelous; how well I know it."

The Lord created you and you are unique! No two people are the same. God sees you as His masterpiece. So, when you look in the mirror, He wants you to know that He is proud of you. Here's a beauty tip: Every morning, look in the mirror and repeat Psalm 139:14 and smile you're biggest and happiest smile.

Proverbs 31:30 – "Churm is deceptive, and beauty does not last; but a woman who fears the Lord will be greatly praised."

Outward beauty fades with age, so if you're most concerned with outer appearance, you'll be unhappy when the wrinkles come, and the scale goes up. Signs of aging begin as early as age twenty. That's why God wants us to "fear" Him. That doesn't mean to be afraid of Him, but rather to be in awe of Him and all that He has done.

1 Timothy 4:8 – "Physical training (exercise) is good, but training for godliness is much better, promising benefits in this life and in the life to come".

Staying in shape is a good thing, but God expects us to stay in shape spiritually by reading our Bibles, praying, and going to church on a regular basis. A person can be physically fit, but if they don't know Jesus Christ, their perfect bodies won't get them through the gates of heaven.

1 Peter 3:3-4 – "Don't be concerned about the outward beauty of fancy hairstyles, expensive jewelry or beautiful clothes. You should cloth yourself instead with the beauty that comes from within, the unfading beauty of a gentle and quite spirit, which is so precious to God".

This doesn't mean that braided hair, nice clothes, and jewelry are wrong. This verse was given to warn women not to follow the customs of some of the Egyptians women who, during that time period, spent hours and hours working on their hair, make-up, and finding the perfect outfit. God would rather see young ladies and women work on becoming beautiful on the inside---the kind of beauty that lasts forever.

One last tip if friends are important to you: Outward beauty can attract superficial friendships, but inner beauty attracts true friends.

26

Polish Your Character to Make Your Personality Shine

"Choose a good reputation over great riches; being held in high esteem is better than silver or gold"
(Proverbs 22:1).

A little polish will make things look very different in this world. Wax and polish will make an old car vastly more attractive. Polish on a pair of dusty shoes will change them from ugliness, to something neat and respectable. I can remember as a child watching my Dad polish and shine his boots and shoes. It's as though his old shoes would renew their youth when they were shined and buffed. When shoes are cleaned like this it's true the shoes are the same kind of shoes they were before and maybe won't last any longer, but they're better to look at and be seen in.

Polish counts a great deal in dealing with the most valuable and important things. This is especially true of diamonds and other precious stones. It takes lots of polishing to make a great diamond blaze with light. When they're first mined, they're often covered with a dark, rusty coating. But the polishing process brings out their beauty and brilliancy.

Sometimes we say about a young boy, "That kid is a diamond in the rough." What we mean is there is a good deal of ability in him and some good qualities of mind and heart, but he's immature and needs to be taught some positive things and how to conduct himself.

My wife and I were attending a basketball game at our local high school one afternoon when out of the blue a young boy came up to us and said, "Hello Bro. Matt. I just wanted to come over, speak and say hello." And with a sure confidence he put his hand out and gave me a good strong hand shake. I was impressed with this young man and how he carried himself with confidence and poise. He wasn't a stranger to me, for he attended our weekly Royal Ambassador (R.A.) meetings at the church where I pastor. This young boy of 10 years is in the process of being polished and certainly will be a positive influence on those who have the privilege of meeting him.

I made the comment to my wife that his parents must be proud of him and that he is a sure product of his parents' teaching and the R.A. program. R.A.s is a mission-education program for school-age boys. The R.A. Pledge goes like this:

"As a Royal Ambassador I will do my best to become a well-informed responsible follower of Christ. To have a Christ-like concern for all people and to learn how the message of Christ is carried around the world; to work with others in sharing Christ and to keep myself clean and healthy in mind and body."

I think boys need to be cautioned about the lack of polish these days. Many young men make the great blunder of getting an entirely erroneous idea of what is manly. Sometimes a boy smokes a cigarette because he thinks it will make him look "manly" or "cool". It makes him look anything but that. You'll hear a boy using blistering, foul words, and sometimes vulgar or profane words because he imagines that it makes him sound rugged, tough, and macho. All of that is the wrong idea of manly. Most people would agree with me when I say that courage, strength, and honesty are robust qualities. But they're even more robust when they're gracefully presented to the world in a kind and courteous manner. 1 Peter 5:5-6 says,

"Young men must accept the authority of the elders. And all of you dress yourselves in humility as you relate to one another, for God opposes the proud but gives grace to the humble. So humble yourselves under the mighty power of God, and at the right time He will lift you up in honor."

Jesus Christ was the one perfect man who has ever

lived. He was frank, truthful, and courteous. His whole conduct showed a marvelous amount of polish. He dealt with all sorts of people in palaces, weddings, funerals, lunches and dinners. He encountered people on fishing trips, in mass meetings, at the church (synagogues). He met people who brought their sick and people possessed with demons for him to heal. Sometimes he was very popular, at other times unpopular, and yet through it all there was a polish of gentleness about him. He had a consideration for others' feelings; a desire to do well and to give happiness.

The sterling qualities of a polished boy include: courage, pluck, fortitude, vigor, bravery, grit, guts, will, truthfulness, kindness, stamina, heart, patience, spirit, determination, and endurance. These and other great, rugged characteristics of your manliness stand out as something beautiful and splendid. Don't be afraid, boys, to put on the polish of true beauty of character. It will not hide your strength; it will only make it shine.

27

The Greatest Fisherman

*"Come, follow me, and I will show you how to fish for people!
And they left their nets at once and followed him"
(Matthew 4:19-20).*

One of my most memorable activities of childhood was fishing with my grandfather. He passed away, but not before we made some fishing memories that are sure to appeal to the most avid angler. There is a fishing story found in a passage from John 21 that always intrigued me as a child and it still has a captivating effect on me.

Some friends had been fishing all night with nothing to show for it. Their minds were perplexed, their bodies tired, and their hearts troubled and disheartened. But when they saw Jesus with a little fire built on the shore, he suddenly called out to them, "Hey, did you fellas catch anything?"

They did not recognize him at first, but answered with a disappointingly, "No!"

He told them to cast the net on the right side of the boat and they would catch a mess of fish. With wonder and speculation, the group of fishermen did as he said, and the net became full of fish. John turned to Peter and said, "It's the Lord that speaks to us!"

Peter jumped overboard and swam ashore to see Jesus. Time and time again, the disciples always caught fish when Jesus was near to them. He often used the net and the fisherman's personal call to "follow him" to illustrate the greater mission of winning souls and capturing them for him. He promised then and it still holds today, that anyone who would follow him, he would make them "fishers of men"; to include women and children too. This is for any Christian who will follow Christ with humility and obedience.

The church is to cast the net among the people in and around them. To do so is to help save them from their sins here and bring them to everlasting glory in heaven. Jesus is the one who saves, and we must bring them to him. During Christ's earthly ministry people were healed and saved when they came in touch with him, and if we are to do our part in saving the people around us, we must bring them in contact with Christ.

When Jesus was here physically, men and women were usually won to Christ through a personal means. The glory of a revival of religion is that it arouses many people to go out personally with the hand net, and talk with different people about Jesus and bring them into contact with him. Then as the people come to the church and listen to the Word, the preacher can cast the larger net in obedience to the Master's command. No other work we can do is so great and glorious as this.

It matters not how big a church is; its members should go forth and intentionally try to influence others to come to Christ by way of their attendance in church. If every church member could only see clearly their duty to this task and the promise of the Spirit to help them, the church would have more influence.

We would probably be surprised of how many successful people in business and the social scene are lonely inside and are filled with an inexpressible longing for peace. Christ is:

"The Prince of Peace" (Isaiah 9:6).

If only we would be so deliberate in casting the net in Jesus' name.

A Christian man sensed God's Spirit leading him to talk with a popular and wealthy community member about his relationship to God and heaven. He did so, but with trepidation not knowing how the man would receive it. At the close of their talk, the man expressed hope that he had not been too bold or impertinent. The distinguished man shook his hand and said, "Don't ever hesitate to speak to any man or woman about their soul. I've longed for 20 years to have a sincere Christian speak to me like you have. I needed to have your questions answered by me. And I believe there are thousands of people in this city who are in the same condition that I am. They are carrying an uneasy conscience and a great burden on their souls; not courageous enough to seek instruction, yet willing to receive it."

Think of those who have been dealing with adversity, misfortune, and sorrow. You have the answer, you have Christ and the abundant life he calls all of us to. Why not share it with those you meet?

A lady who volunteered at a homeless shelter once had a conversation with a transient. During their conversation, she let no opportunity slip to put in an occasional word about her Lord. She told him about Jesus. She had been kind to him; non-judgmental and he saw Jesus in her eyes and face. After he had his meal, he thanked her and left to go find work. He came by three days later and told her he was still looking for work. Again, she pointed him to Christ. She heard nothing more from him until six months later. A letter came to the shelter addressed to her. He explained that he had found steady employment, had an apartment, but most of all, found Christ as his personal Savior. He was happy and hoped to be living a useful

Christian life. He assured her that he owed his salvation to her kindness to him and faithful words she had spoken to him about Christ.

The opportunities of casting a net for Jesus are all around us when we're ready to work in harmony with our Lord. Christ expects us to help him in the salvation of souls for whom we're praying. There's a place for all of us in God's Kingdom, even in our own prayers. For when we pray we open a channel in which God can speak to us. For all of us, hundreds of opportunities have come and gone. Talking about the weather, the latest news, politics, sports, and business are all well and good, but to neglect a word about what God has done for you is simply a missed opportunity. Are you doing your duty as a friend of Jesus Christ, to offer the Good News of the Gospel? May God help you to not forget to cast the net wherever Christ says to go throw it.

28

Strength and Confidence Found in Christ

"I can do all things through Christ who gives me strength"
(Philippians 4:13).

The best evidence of the Resurrection of Christ is the fact he has the power to pull people out of the sloughs of despondency, to lift us up out of the mire and clay of sin. His power places our feet upon the rock and gives us new reasons to thank and praise Him. Every person that's lifted into this new life are evidences of Christianity. This becomes their personal testimony to life. Christianity, in general must always be judged by the kind of people it makes. It's a matter of looking to Jesus always. The Bible says, in Acts 7:55-56,

"Stephen, being full of the Holy Spirit, gazed steadily into heaven and saw Jesus standing at God's right hand."

The apostle Paul declares that if we are risen with

Christ and have followed him up out of the grave, as Stephen did, then we will be inspired to live a noble life. This life will be of high thought and pure imagination in a way that we can touch the world with the helpfulness of Christ. Some people tend to dwell on the fact the Christian life is complete self-sacrifice and self-denial. The surrendered life to Christ gives you something better than what you have lost for Christ's sake. When a person gives their heart to God's purpose, Christ raises them to a higher place. And it is true Christ's standards are higher than the worlds. It makes practical sense that we need him to help us meet his standards. When we accept Christ as our Savior and Lord, we are in the glorious position to receive his aid. The Bible says,

"We are partners together with God,"
(1 Corinthians 3:9).

Christ has paid the price and raised us to a mighty and lofty status. Revelation 1:5-6 says,

"Jesus Christ the faithful witness, the first to rise from the dead and the ruler of all the kings of the world. He loves us and has freed us from our sins by shedding his blood for us. He has made us a Kingdom of priests for God his Father. All glory and power to him forever and ever. Amen!"

We can be sure that whatever Christ promised in his Word, or whatever he has done for others in the Bible, he is able to do for us. We can also be certain that no commandments are given to us that he will not help us achieve and obey.

A young officer had orders from his commander to assault an enemy's position that had been considered impregnable. A fellow officer told him, "It can't be taken, and you'll lose your life!"

The brave Soldier replied, "I can, because I have the order in my pocket." And take it he did. Always remember there's nothing to which God has commanded us in His Word, or to which the Holy Spirit directs us in our daily life, that we cannot do in Jesus' name.

The highest and noblest life that a person can ever hope to live is possible to each of us if we walk in fellowship with Jesus Christ. Our duty is to stay in touch with Christ through prayer, worship, and fellowship. We are to live in an atmosphere where prayer will be so natural to us that it becomes a regular source of nourishment and strength.

A teenager was eating a snack in the kitchen of his home. He noticed his mother's "To Do List" laying on the counter. It was the typical items: wash clothes, mop kitchen, go to grocery store, pick-up kids from school, dry clothes, fix supper, fold clothes, put up clothes, water the flowers. But one thing stood out from the rest, sandwiched in between going to the grocery store and getting the kids were the three words "Read and Pray". Then he saw what made her a wonderful Mom. He knew why with all her burdens she was sweet-spirited, self-composed, and always able to give counsel, comfort, and cheer to those who were discouraged, including himself. Prayer was a regular source of strength for her and Bible reading kept her focused so she could live, function, and even help others to thrive on a higher plane in life. No person can live the risen life in his or her own strength. The risen life is sustained by looking to Jesus.

Hebrews 12:2 reminds us to:

"Run with endurance the race God has set before us. We do this by keeping our eyes on Jesus, the champion who perfects our faith."

We are to look to Jesus in four ways:

Look to Jesus "In" everything (Acts 17:28). In good times as well as bad, in joy as well as sorrow, and in triumph as well as trial we must look to Jesus. Doing so will help us obtain mercy and find grace to help in every time of need.

Second, look to Jesus "For" everything. Relying on self-effort alone will lead us to disappointment. "According to His riches in glory by Christ Jesus" (Philippians 4:19) all our needs will be met.

Third, look to Jesus "With" everything. If we are to be overcomers and victorious in life, we must look to Jesus with everything and that includes our time, talent, and treasure. The apostle Paul urges us to "Present our bodies to God as a living sacrifice" (Romans 12:1), so that we may be totally dedicated to Him.

Finally, look to Jesus "Through" everything. When traveling through all phases of life, even the valley experiences, God will often allow suffering to strengthen our faith and fulfill His purpose. Don't complain and blame God when suffering strikes, rather look to Him and seek His purpose with patience and trust.

Let God resurrect your spirits, with the same power Christ was resurrected on that glorious Easter morning so many years ago!

How to Look to Jesus

- ◆ IN everything.
- ◆ FOR everything.
- ◆ WITH everything.
- ◆ THROUGH everything.

29

If You Seek Peace, You Can Find It

Spring is a time of renewal and can bring refreshing inspirations into our lives. The unexpected inspirations can be the best of all. Years ago, one of those times occurred three days after celebrating Easter with my family. I had military orders to report to an assignment in a northern state. It was a short-term mission of 16 days and I would have access to well over 1,000 military personnel. My counseling ranged from family issues, stress related circumstances, relationships, faith questions, medical, personal and general battlefield stress. Knowing I could help care for more if I went to them, rather than wait for them to come to me, I decided to do some battlefield circulation on the main post where a few operational units were tied to tasks at their work stations.

I stopped into the Joint Operations Center and started talking to a young sergeant who commenced to tell me how tasked out she was with the mission and things happening with her family back home. She shared with me how much she missed her daughter, especially having to leave so soon after Easter. I told her I understood and affirmed that she had a duty there and a duty to be here; a challenging position to be in.

She responded, "You know Chaplain, I'm doing better than I thought I would and here's why. Right before I left home to go to the airport I opened a box of Easter candy that had chocolate rabbits in it. The "Serenity Prayer" was printed on the inside flap. You know the one that says: God grant me the serenity to accept the things I cannot change; courage to change the things I can; and wisdom to know the difference? I simply tore that small part of the box and placed it in my pocket and brought it with me. And occasionally I'll take it out and read it. It helps me with the concerns at home and it's helping me to stay focused on our mission here. I've got peace about all of it. Thank goodness for Easter candy and God's promises!"

I told her how inspirational her story was and to be sure to share it when she sees someone else needing a spirit lifter.

Even amid the most trying and taxing circumstances,

God's peace can be attained. Jesus' own words were,

"Peace is what I leave with you, it is my own peace that I give you. I do not give it as the world does. Do not be worried or upset, do not be afraid" (John 14:27).

Even Christians are prone to becoming troubled and disheartened in life's circumstances. It's not easy to live successfully in this world, and it's impossible to not be affected by the world's chaotic and superficial ways. But Christians need not crawl around on their hands and knees and tell the world how awful life is and how things are bad all over. You can experience the peace and serenity that Christ desires for you to have. The steps to achieving peace in your life include these six things:

Think peaceful thoughts. Many people lack God's peace because they continue to think stressful and fearful thoughts. They think fear thoughts instead of faith thoughts. God tells us He will keep in perfect peace, those whose mind is focused on Him (Isaiah 26:3). We must surrender our tension and fears to God and claim His promises and the peace of God, which is beyond human understanding will guard your hearts (Philippians 4:7).

See peaceful sights. We must counter the temptation to follow the footsteps of others by watching violent scenes, destructive tactics, and the glorification of death on the TV and movie screens. If we are to live by peace, we must look to Jesus who gives us the peace we seek.

Hear peaceful sounds. The Bible says faith comes by hearing (Romans 10:17). So, if we fill our ears with the world's noise through constant lewd, loud, and languishing music our spiritual nerves will get depleted trying to counteract it. To enjoy peace, we need to temper our listening with wholesome, uplifting music even in the natural setting. Listening to the wind blow through the trees or hearing the waves crash against the sea shore promotes serenity and peace in effective ways.

Speak peaceful words. The tongue can be destructive concerning peace. A Christian needs to talk about the goodness of the Lord instead of criticizing and finding fault. To experience peace we must speak kindly, remembering that:

"A gentle answer quiets anger, but a harsh one stirs it up. Kind words bring life, but cruel words crush your spirit" (Proverbs 15:1,4).

Perform peaceful deeds. You don't have to go far from your front door to find needy people in today's world. Some are sick, elderly, and unable to care for themselves. Peace is a by-product for those who lend a helping hand to others. There's no excuse for a person, especially a Christian who claims to follow Christ, to not help others. Everyone can comfort someone. Whenever you can, do good to help those who need it (Proverbs 3:27).

Attend peaceful places. We bring trouble upon ourselves by going to places not intended for us. The free will God gives us can be liberating, but it's dangerous. We must be wise about where our feet take us. We must be watchful about the places we frequent. Where we go, God should be glorified, not nullified.

The Soldier I met at the Operations Center attended chapel services and there was a peaceful countenance on her face. Peace, however, is more than skin deep. Peace will affect every part of your life, inside and out. Accept the peace that Christ offers you.

How to Achieve Peace in Your Life

- Think peaceful thoughts.
- See peaceful sights.
- Hear peaceful sounds.
- Speak peaceful words.
- Perform peaceful deeds.
- Attend peaceful places.

30

When Life Wears You Out

*"Come to me, all of you who are weary and carry heavy
burdens, and I will give you rest"
(Matthew 11:28).*

While on a military assignment on the west coast of
the United States I had the opportunity to meet and greet
several hundred Soldiers. One day while making my
rounds through the base, I met one young man who had
been working a 14-hour shift at his job. I asked him, "It
was 110 degrees out there today. How are you doing?"

"Not too good Chaplain, not too good," he responded.

I wanted more insight into his trouble, so I asked him
another question, "Not too good, physically, emotionally,
or spiritually?"

He said, "All of the above!"

So, I told him, "I don't have all the answers, but I can
offer some suggestions for all three. For the physical, get
to bed early. Rest is as good as medicine. For the emo-

tional part, don't think you have to get it all done in one day. A little bit each shift will help keep it from overwhelming you. As far as the spiritual side of the house, meditate on this good Word, He (God) gives power to the weak and strength to the powerless (Isaiah 40:29).

I wrote the verse on one of my cards, gave it to him, and said, "Just call it your prescription for soul care."

This young Soldier isn't the only one searching for strength to make it through the day. We all are! When we're young we feel invincible. Yet, even when we're young we get tired. As young, inexperienced people, we try to make our way in the world, then we get tired, stumble, and fall. We experience failures in all areas. We discover we don't have all the answers, and we're not as smart as we thought. And we think to ourselves, maybe I do need somebody to help make life work for me. The reality of it all is that whatever stage of life we find ourselves, God's strength is enough to sustain us. The surest way to gain strength for what you need to accomplish is through a characteristic I like to call "spiritual resiliency".

Spirituality is a dimension of personal wellness everyone needs to practice to a functional capacity through the ups and downs of life. Spirituality for the Christian helps you feel connected to the Higher Power, something bigger than yourself. And it builds resilience at the same time.

Spirituality involves beliefs and values that contribute

to your purpose for living. The tip of the iceberg for spiritual resiliency rests in the strength of an individual's relationship with God. The benefits of knowing God and seeking Him helps you by promoting healthy connections with others, increasing your chances of making healthier lifestyle choices, and promoting strength to endure hard times. It also increases the effectiveness of your witness.

I can personally guarantee you increased strength for every day of your life if you genuinely do the following four things:

There's strength through PRAYER to God. Show me a weak Christian spiritually, and I'll show you a person with a poor prayer life. Prayer is the Christian's lifeline. Through prayer we communicate and fellowship with God. Genuine daily prayer is like stopping at a gas station because your vehicle is almost empty; you fill up your tank and keep on driving. Fellowship with God fills your love tank.

Strength can be gained emotionally, through the PROMISES of God. The apostle Paul called them "exceedingly precious promises" (2 Peter 1:4). God says,

"I will strengthen you and help you. I will hold you up with my victorious (righteous) hand" (Isaiah 41:10).

Everyone, young and old, great and small will benefit by seeking out the promises in God's Word. There's a promise to fit every personal need. Remember them, recall them often, and claim them as your own.

Labor in the Lord always produces a positive return. Therefore, physical strength can be gained by PERFORMING God's Work. There's a divine energy that's as real as any endorphin rush through your body. It's called the rush of the Holy Spirit, and it surges through your soul. There's a song a lady used to sing in church titled: "Holy Spirit Flow Through Me". God promises:

"Power to the faint, and to them that have no might he increases strength" (Isaiah 40:29).

Spiritually, a person gains strength as they PRAISE God and worship Him. In Psalm 71, after saying he would praise the Lord more and more, the psalmist said,

"I will go in the strength of the Lord."

Praise encourages a positive attitude and lifts our sagging spirits. Just remember to keep your feet on the ground but let your heart soar as high as you can dream. Refuse to be average or give into spiritual ignorance. Trust God and soar above life's challenges with strength.

How to Get Strength for Each New Day

- Strength through prayer to God.
- Strength through the promises of God.
- Strength by performing God's work.
- Strength by praising God.

31

God Hears Your Prayers

"The eyes of the Lord watch over those who do right, and His ears are open to their prayers"
(1 Peter 3:12).

A long time ago, a preacher in an England mission hall noticed a great broad-shouldered Sailor come in and sit down in the back of the congregation. After the service was over, the sailor approached one of the ushers and asked, "Do you think the preacher would speak privately with me?"

"Of course, he'll talk to you," the usher assured him.

The usher led the young Sailor to the preacher's study room. When the preacher entered the room, the Sailor began to tell his story:

"I had no thought of being here tonight, preacher. I haven't been living up to what my mother taught me. I left home and my mother almost three years ago. She's a widow and I was her only child. I haven't been as bad as

154

some of my Sailor mates. Believe me, I've tried to run away from her and all the prayers she keeps praying. I've never written, nor sent her any money, even though I've made some good wages. I've even tried to make myself drunk to rid myself of uneasy thoughts. But as I came down the street past the hall, the songs I heard being sung were songs I heard growing up. I used to be in a choir back home. I wanted to come in and sing them again in a church like old times. But I wasn't dressed properly, and I needed a shower. It was just an excuse, preacher. It would have been very easy to give into the devil's easy excuses that he gave me. But somehow, I could not completely walk away. I've never felt a draw that strong before. The devil told me to forget it and just come back next week. But it was no use, before I knew it I was up the steps, through the door, and sitting down in the congregation. It was your preaching that kept me here; your message from the Lord was calling my soul and I heard it. God wanted me, I heard Him, and he softened my heart. If He can help me with this guilt, I'll be a good lad, and go home to mother."

The attentive preacher talked and prayed with the Sailor until, by faith, the young man accepted Christ as His Savior and Lord. As he shook the preacher's hand he said, "I've got a peace inside now; like I used to have when I was young. But this time I know what it is, and I understand it. I'll never be the same as I used to be! I can hardly wait to go and see my mother next Saturday".

Just four days later the same preacher was conducting a service in a smaller town many miles away, and during his sermon he told of the big Sailor's conversion. As he came down from the pulpit he was met by a humble old woman who asked him if he knew the name of the Sailor, and when he told her she exclaimed, "I thought so! That's my boy!"

The dear old mother told the minister how on the previous Sunday she had been thinking very strongly and more than usual about her wandering son. She decided to attend the evening service despite the very bad weather conditions. She had only a thin jacket and her steps were feeble. She had gone about half the distance when she encountered a heavy storm of rain and sleet, so she stopped at a friend's house for shelter. Her friend also happened to be a widow and was a woman of strong faith.

After some conversation, her friend said, "Since it's impossible for either one of us to attend public worship tonight, let's have our own little prayer meeting right here in my house".

She went on to propose their subject of prayer should be for the mother's son. And at that very hour, in a city many miles away, the prodigal son was led to God's house, and while his old mother earnestly prayed, he was saved.

God has given us the great charge of praying on behalf of others. Matthew 18:19 clearly states, "If two of you agree here on earth concerning anything you ask, my Father in heaven will do it for you. For where two or three gathers together as my followers, I am there among them."

Shall we not be one another's lifeline? Shall we not pray for one another's most sincere requests? What a privilege it is to pray on behalf of someone and to know the Power Source that can move mountains is concerned about what matters to each of us. Therefore, let us approach God's throne with bold and confident prayers (Hebrews 4:16); humbly seeking Him in all that is a concern to us. For God's promises will not waver and He wants to give good things to us.

What is there today in your life that needs committed, genuine prayer? Is there someone for whom you are burdened? God says,

"Cry out to me, call upon my name, pray to Me and I will answer. I will be with you, rescue you, and give you my salvation" (Psalm 91:15-16).

32

A Light for Our Darkest Moments

"God is light; in Him there is no darkness at all. So, if we walk in the light, as He is in the light we have fellowship with one another"
(1 John 1:5,7).

A little boy was afraid of the dark. One night his mother told him to go out to the back porch and bring her the broom. The little boy turned to his mother and said, "Momma, I don't want to go out there. It's dark."

The mother smiled reassuringly at her son. "You don't have to be afraid of the dark," she explained, "Jesus is out there. He'll look after you and protect you."

The little boy looked at his mother real hard and asked, "Are you sure he's out there?"

"Yes, I'm sure. He is everywhere, and he's always ready to help you when you need him," she said

The little boy thought about that for a minute and then

went to the back door and cracked it a little. Peering out into the darkness, he called, "Jesus, if you're out there, would you please hand me the broom?"

The Bible differentiates between light and dark in many passages. Jesus called himself "The light of the world" and he said,

"If you follow me, you won't have to walk in darkness, because you will have the light that leads to life," (John 8:12).

Earlier in the gospel of John it says,

"And the judgment is based on this fact: God's light came into the world, but people loved the darkness more than the light, for their actions were evil. All who do evil hate the light and refuse to go near it for fear their sins will be exposed. But those who do what is right come to the light so others can see that they are doing what God wants" (John 3:18-21).

We will be judged according to our light and God will be entirely just with us. If we are condemned before him, it will be because, having seen the light and known the better way, we refused to enter that way and turned our faces toward the darkness. A person who refuses to become a Christian, doesn't by self-will, believe certain Christian truths. To believe in Christ is to know the truth according to God. And the truth hurts the self-will of the unbeliever.

Take the case of "doubting Thomas". He was in the

first group of friends of Jesus when Christ lived on earth. When the other disciples came and told Thomas about the resurrection of Christ, he didn't believe it. He thought they had been deceived. Yet his heart was heavy, and he really wished it were true. Later when Jesus reappeared to all the disciples at one time, rather than scold Thomas, Jesus accepted him and said, "Look at my hands. Put your hand into the wound in my side. Don't be faithless any longer. Believe!" Thomas' doubts were vanquished, and Jesus said,

"You believe because you've seen me. Blessed are those who believe without seeing me" (John 20:27-29).

It's belief that shines light on our circumstances.

We have a very different case in the men that stoned the apostle Stephen to death. The men that murdered Stephen believed what he said about Jesus (Acts 7). The light from heaven had shone upon their eyes, but the light condemned them, and they would not have it, they would not accept it. In that trying moment, Stephen looked upward, and the heavenly world was opened to his eyes. He saw God and Jesus at His right hand. He dismissed the cruel taunts and the stinging blows and said, "Look, I see the heavens opened and the Son of Man (Jesus), Lord Jesus, receive my spirit." And those men, looking on Stephen's face, believed it. They knew he was looking into heaven, for they saw light in his face brighter than any light of earth. But they couldn't yield to the fact that he saw Christ, for that meant condemnation to them. And so, they did what many people have been doing ever since—they "stopped their ears, put their hands over them and ran upon him" as if to silence what he had to say. They sought to extinguish the light for they cared more for the darkness. Our testimony is the light that people see in our lives.

A prosperous man had a Christian wife that prayed for his conversion. He was lying awake in the darkness of his room one night, when he heard the voice from a little bed that was beside his.

"Papa, it's so dark, take my hand."

He took the little hand extended in the dark and held it gently until the frightened child fell-fast asleep. This strong, proud, business man looked up through the darkness, and said, "Father, in heaven, it is dark. Will you take my hand as I took my own dear child's hand? Give me rest of soul for Jesus' sake."

A blessed peace entered his broken heart, and quietly amid the darkness he rejoiced in salvation. A very small beam of light had come to him in his child's appeal. The sense of helpless weakness had led him to stretch the hand of his soul up to God, and Jesus Christ. God took hold and saved him in that moment. Trust God for the light that leads to salvation and faith. Lift your hand into the darkness today, trusting God through Jesus Christ, and he will take hold of you and save you, for this is what Christ was born to do—to save us! If you refuse this light which he offers and you turn from it, there is yet a deeper darkness that is yet to come for you that can only mean greater sorrow as the years go on. Follow the light which God gives you and it will lead you to heaven. It doesn't take a great deal of light, to lead heavenward the one who is willing to be led.

33

When You Need a Helping Hand

"Don't be afraid, for I am with you. Don't be discouraged, for I am your God. I will strengthen you and help you. I will hold you up with my victorious right hand"
(Isaiah 41:10).

While traveling through the southeastern state of Virginia recently, I stopped in a quaint little town for lunch. It was a small town with an easy-going spirit. It reminded me of my home town of Jay because of the neighborly friendliness. Even the attendant at the local gas station had a happy face.

I bypassed the typical fast-food chains for lunch and opted for a little restaurant called the "Farmer's Café". A sign above the front door said, "Come enjoy some country cookin'!" So, I did. After a satisfying meal I went to the front of the building to pay. A family stood up to leave at the same time as me and a little girl, probably 4-5 years-old, jumped up from their table and beat me to the cashier. As I prepared to pay, the waitress asked the little girl jokingly, "So, where's your money? You must pay for your food too. It's not free!"

"Well, I don't have any money," the little girl replied.

With a quick wink at me, the cashier said, "Looks like you're gonna need some help paying for your lunch."

Just then, the little girl turned and saw her grandfather walking up beside her. She looked back at the cashier with confidence and a straight face and said, "It's alright now. I don't have any money, but I have my Grandpa's money." A grandfather saves the day and the little girl had full confidence he would pay her lunch ticket.

I'm reminded each day how our heavenly Father paid the sin debt for all of us. And there isn't a day that goes by in which we don't need His help in managing life and knowing how to live. Psalm 91:1-2 says,

"Those who live in the shelter of the Highest (God) will find rest in the shadow of the Almighty. He alone is my refuge, my place of safety, He is my God, and I trust Him."

Knowing that God loves us like He does, we can count the many ways He helps us.

One such way is by God's presence. As a family you can enjoy time together. As a Christian with brothers and sisters in Christ, you can enjoy time in the family of God. Fellowship awaits us in the presence of God. We should practice welcoming His presence into our life. He is with us every day, every hour, and every moment. And we are as close to Him and our fellow believers as we want to be.

We also gain God's power as a help for living. He has proven His omnipotence by creating the heavens and the earth. There exists no greater power than that of the divine. He will never tire from helping us and is abundantly able to meet all our needs. He can change people and the circumstances they are in. His power knows no limits.

God's providence also helps us by giving divine guidance through His loving care and intervention. Providence means: "the act of providing". I Corinthians 10:13 says,

"God is faithful. He will not allow the temptation to be more than you can stand. When you are tempted, He will show you a way out so that you can endure."

God always provides an escape from temptation. It's there, but we must look for it. He directs and intervenes in unusual ways.

God's protection is best illustrated in the words of Psalm 91:10-11 where it says,

"No evil will conquer you; for He will order His angels to protect you wherever you go."

Distance is not a problem for God. Through our prayers, He reaches down to protect our families, friends, loved ones, and the missionaries in foreign lands.

It's also God's promises that give us aid in life. His promises are great, and they are certainly many. God's promises do not fail, because He cannot fail. Hebrews 10:23 says,

> *"As we hold firmly to faith and hope, God can be trusted to keep His promises."*

This means we must meet the conditions He has set before the promises can be ours.

God has an irresistible love for His children and because of it, He wants to help us. The Bible does not say God will help those who help themselves, but it does say,

> *"God will help those who depend on Him"*
> *(Lamentations 3:25).*

The more we love God, the more faithfully we serve Him, the truer we are to His worship, the deeper we long for heaven, the more magnetism there will be for His help. If we keep an open heart and home for God's angels, we may dwell in dark places of hardship here on earth, but we can know the darkness of this world and the earthly tents we pitch are temporary.

Just as the little girl from Virginia trusted fully with no doubt that her Grandpa would help her, let us trust fully in God's presence, power, providence, protection, and promises. Every day's march is one step nearer to our abiding rest.

<u>How God Helps Us</u>

- ◆ His Presence.

- ◆ His Power.

- ◆ His Providence.

- ◆ His Protection.

- ◆ His Promises.

34

Promises That Are Never Broken

*"God keeps His promises for a thousand generations and lav-
ishes His unfailing love on those who love Him and obey His
commands"*
(Deuteronomy 7:9)

The two most common areas of struggle for us are work and relationships. We can all relate to these common everyday struggles. Job 5:7 speaks of this truth when it says,

"People are born for trouble as readily as sparks fly up from a fire."

We struggle at times to make a living, because our jobs often present challenges to overcome. And sometimes our jobs don't pay as much as we think we need. For some people, it can be hard to even find good work. Because of the sins committed in the Garden of Eden, God said,

"The ground is cursed because of you. All your life you will

struggle to scratch a living from it" (Genesis 3:17).

We also tend to struggle in our relationships. Marriage, while it can be a great blessing, it's not always easy. Parenting, though rewarding, can push us to the limit too. And being a good friend sometimes requires us to make great sacrifices.

Even though life is difficult, God's promises are enough to sustain us. 2 Peter 1:3-4 says,

"By his divine power, God has given us everything we need for living a godly life. We have received all of this by coming to know Him, the one who called us to Himself by means of His marvelous glory and excellence. And because of His glory and excellence, He has given us great and precious promises".

So many times, people will fail to keep their promises causing hurt and disappointments. But God's promises are always kept. Although we don't always understand His ways and why He allows certain circumstances to affect us, we can be assured He will never let us down. As hard as life can be at times consider the following eight "P-R-O-M-I-S-E-S" we have from God:

Peace of mind: Peace in today's world is practically unknown. Greed, suspicion, lack of brotherly love, and hunger for power prevent us from experiencing real and lasting peace. God promises peace of mind and heart to those who trust Him. Proof:

"You (God) will keep in perfect peace all who trust in you, all whose thoughts are fixed on you!" (Isaiah 26:3).

Rest from labor: We live in a restless age of much "busy-ness" and little leisure or "time to live". There're always more things we think we need to do. Jesus promised rest from the strain and worry of life if we will cast our cares on Him and wait patiently for Him. Proof:

"Come to me, all of you who are tired from carrying heavy loads, and I will give you rest" (Matthew 11:28).

Opportunity for service: Our selfish interests too often deter us from walking through God's door of opportunity to be "workers with Him". When we take time to do God's work, He has promised to supply the strength, courage, and opportunity. Proof:

"I have opened a door in front of you, which no one can close" (Revelation 3:8).

Mercy in need: Because we are human, we're going to make blunders. Even as Christians we will flounder many times. But God's mercy is available to reinstate us. God promises grace to help in time of need. He forgives and cleanses us when we confess our sins and commit our lives to Christ. Proof:

"Let us have confidence, then, and approach God's throne, where there is grace. There we will receive mercy and find grace to help us just when we need

it" (Hebrews 4:16).

Instructions for direction: It's important to understand that God's promises are of no avail to people who are set in their own ways and reject God's instruction. Earnest Christians welcome God's instruction, knowing His direction is always best. God has promised to lead; we need only to follow. Proof:

"The Lord says, I will teach you the way you should go; I will instruct you and advise you" (Psalm 32:8).

Strength in weakness: Our strength is finite, limited, and often fails, but God's infinite power never fails. So why do we persist in depending on our own limitations. Little children become aware of their lack of strength because that's why they depend on their parents. Our heavenly parent promises strength to His trusting children. Proof:

"I am your God. I will strengthen you and help you" (Isaiah 41:10).

Escape in temptation: When Jesus himself was tempted in the wilderness, He used the Word of God to defeat Satan. We need to do the same. God promises victory in temptation to those who use His Word and pray. Proof:

"God keeps His promises; when you are tested; He will provide you with a way out" (1 Corinthians 10:13).

Security for the future: Unbelievers will seek security

in power, pleasure, and possessions, but it's Christ alone who gives real and lasting security. One day for believers there will be no more sin, sickness, suffering, or sorrow, for the former things will be passed away. Proof:

Jesus said, "I go to prepare a place for you; I will come again and get you so that you will be where I am"
(John 14:2-13).

You can have confidence that no matter what life throws at you, God's grace is enough to sustain you. Believe His promises. He is faithful.

<u>Promises We Have from God</u>

P-eace of Mind

R-est from Labor

O-pportunities for Service

M-ercy in Need

I-nstructions for Directions.

S-rength in Weakness

E-scape in Temptations

S-ecurity for the Future

35

Mother's Love is Divine and True

"Children are a gift from the Lord; they are a reward"
(Psalm 127:3).

After a hard-fought battle during the Civil War, a Confederate Chaplain was called to see a dying Soldier. Taking his hand, he asked, "My brother, what can I do for you?" He supposed that like many other wounded Soldiers; he wanted him to plead with God to spare his life and take the pain away. But this young fellow was different.

"Chaplain," he said, "I want you to cut a lock of hair for my mother. And then chaplain, I want you to kneel down and return thanks for me."

"I can do that. But what is it your thankful for?" asked the chaplain.

"For my mother--she's been so good to me. Her teachings are my comfort. Because of her loving influence and teachings, I'm now a Christian, and I'm able to look up into Heaven and say, Our Father who art in Heaven. What would I do now if I weren't a Christian? And Chaplain, thank Him for my promised home in glory. I'll soon be there to wait on mother and to welcome her."

And so, the chaplain knelt by the side of the Soldier's death-cot, not to utter a word to spare his life, but only to echo through prayer the praise and thanksgiving of a dying young boy for a good mother, a Christian hope, dying grace, and an eternal home in Heaven.

It's this thought of God, as One who loves us personally, that we should give thanks for. As our hearts respond faithfully in obedience and gratitude our thoughts of a great God are transformed. We can say tenderly, "My God and my salvation. For this I am thankful".

Our mothers are known for making things better. As a child, we cry out for her when we fall and scrap our knee. As we grow in wisdom and stature we learn to trust in God and we instinctively cry out to God who can make all things right within our soul. We have in a mother's love a figure which God has used to make Himself known to us It's a suggestion of the sacrificial love which caused Him to come to our rescue when we were poor sinners. How thankful are we for this life saving action? There is no other illustration that can come so near, adequately picturing that compassion and love which is revealed in the statement of Jesus:

"God so loved the world that He gave His only begotten Son, that whosoever believeth in Him should not perish, but have everlasting life" (John 3:16).

How like the mother's heart, is the tenderness of God. That He seeks after us in our sins, and continues to do so, though we wonder off in our own ways. How thankful we should be for this alone! God's provision is what helps us to endure the struggles we face. Blessings come and go, but the love of God, despite our waywardness is an anchor for our soul. It's the greatest blessing!

The person that refuses to move because of God's love is perhaps the hardest thing in the world to understand. Those who grit their teeth and turn from the glory of the One that created them yield themselves to an indifferent world that actively works to destroy their life and their spirit to live.

There's perfect restfulness and peace found in the motherhood of God.

"God is our defender and refuge, and an ever-present help in times of trouble" (Psalm 46:1).

If a child has anything it wants to keep, something that's precious and it wants to be sure that it's defended against all comers, it turns to its mother. Mothers are great treasure-keepers. So, if we will give our hearts to God in grateful obedience, we know that He will keep it safe. He has the strength, wisdom, and love to keep forever what we commit to His hands.

This can be the personal theme for us throughout our life. A person doesn't have to keep on living with a vague and indifferent idea about God, Christ, Heaven, and the immortal life. I call you to something infinitely more precious than that. God loves you with the tenderness of a mother's heart. In your loneliness, in your sorrow, in your cries for help remember the words of Isaiah 66:13:

"I (God) will comfort you as a mother comforts her child."

In your thanksgiving this season, whether you're sorrowful or sinful or not feeling very thankful because of losses in your life, count the blessings of God—name them one by one. There's infinite compassion and love to be found. Find forgiveness in Him and you will feel the power of thanksgiving grow stronger and stronger within you.

36

Don't Waste the Wilderness Experiences

"These trials will show that your faith is genuine. It is being tested as fire tests and purifies gold. So, when your faith remains strong through many trials, it will bring you much praise and glory when Christ is revealed to the whole world"
(1 Peter 1:7).

A Soldier once shared with me a wilderness journey he experienced in life. It was one in which he found a way through and God provided for him. I met him on a military assignment in a southern state. He had been deployed several years earlier and was now preparing for another one. He explained that during his first deployment his wife was unfaithful with his so-called best friend. He cried all night; for days. After a week of this he decided to pray about it. He would cry and pray, pray and cry and this routine continued for a week. On the seventh day he developed a peace that he could not explain. When he returned home from his deployment, his wife left him. While the divorce papers were being processed through the court, she asked him, "Aren't you going to try and get revenge?"

To her surprise, he said, "No, I have to pay for my sins and you have to pay for yours."

He went on to tell me, "God blessed me with another wife, a better wife, and if that wasn't enough, He blessed me with two kids. I am very happy now."

I said, "Brother, you went through the wilderness, but managed to survive. Many people would have gotten lost in that circumstance and given up."

"Well, I knew I had to keep living. In life, to get where you need to go, you must run sometimes and walk at other times. It's what you do to get the thrill of living!"

Sometimes life takes us down a pathway into the wilderness and we look around one day and ask ourselves how did I get here? Why am I here? Many, many years ago that very thing happened to Elijah. 1 Kings 17:2-7 says,

"Then the Lord said to Elijah, go to the east and hide by Kerith Brook, near where it enters the Jordan River. Drink from the brook and eat what the ravens bring you. For I have commanded them to bring you food. So, Elijah did as the Lord told him and camped beside Kerith Brook. The ravens brought him bread and meat each morning and evening and

he drank from the brook. But after a while the brook dried up, for there was no rainfall anywhere in the land."

Despite the wilderness circumstances, God wants all of us to enjoy life through Him. Resentment, unforgiveness, and hate stop the flow of God's supply to you. You need to be filled with His Spirit every day. We must want God, seek God, and trust Him to provide for our needs!

On one of my visits to the Blue Ridge Mountains in North Carolina I wanted to survey the little town I was staying in. So, I started to drive and noticed a road sign that said: "Road to No Where". It's a sad place to be, but we all pass by there sooner or later. That's when we turn our battles over to the Lord. 2 Chronicles 20:15-17 reads,

"This is what the Lord says, do not be afraid! Don't be discouraged by this mighty army, for the battle is not yours, but God's. Tomorrow march out against your enemies (your struggles). You will find them coming up through the wilderness. Take your positions; watch the Lord's victory. He is with you, do not be afraid or discouraged. Go out against them tomorrow, for the Lord is with you!"

It seems only when our wisdom and strength fail are we willing to turn the problem over to Him. Instead of giving way to despair, it's our privilege and right to go to God at the outset during our difficulties, as well as in all conditions. What a comfort it is to know that God is at our side in fair weather or in the storms.

It's a delight for God to fellowship with us no matter how difficult the path or how rugged the wilderness becomes. It's our surrender and reliance upon Him during the trial that He is seeking from us. Don't waste the wilderness but use it as Elijah did when he was there. There are four things to do when you find yourself feeling alone because of your troubles: 1) Learn to recognize the provisions of God. God can and will provide for your needs (Philippians 4:19); 2) Appreciate God's blessings. Give thanks for God and all that He has done for you in the past (Psalm 126:3); 3) Make good use of what God gives you. It may not be in the form you thought, but God knows best what you need (Philippians 2:13); 4) Embrace where God places you. Everything has a season and a purpose, so make the most of your opportunities, no matter where He leads you (1 Corinthians 7:17).

Blessings rarely drive us to God; it's usually crisis that do it. It's when the crises of life are reached that our Lord shows Himself "a mighty present help". The experience of darkness, of prayers seemingly unanswered, of sin which seems triumphant, and of affliction; these are the channels through which we often learn how truly great our God is! If you allow the Spirit to be active and alive in your life, you can do something about your problems. Don't waste the wilderness, but let God lead you through it and onward to victory!

37

Navigating Through God's Purposes for You

"Trust in the Lord with all your heart; do not depend on your own understanding. Seek His will in all you do, and He will show you which path to take"
(Proverbs 3:5-6).

Do you ever question God's purpose and will for your life? Or in your later years, do you wonder if you have accomplished what God wanted you to do? One of the great statements ever made of a person can be found in Luke 2:52,

"Jesus grew in wisdom and in stature and in favor with God and all the people."

Living a purposeful and committed life requires devotion to the mission in which you were created.

In my 25 years in the ministry, most all of it has been in a bi-vocational capacity. I have had to learn that it's not my full-time job and preaching on the side. I have realized in time that my business was to be then and is now, preaching the gospel. I work secular jobs to pay my expenses. Everyone ought to consider their secular employment as only the means for earning a living, so that your focus, if you're a Christian, is to give yourself to the work of Christ and building God's Kingdom. It's important to have full-time religious workers, but if the world is ever to be won to Christ, it will be the rank-and-file Christians, who take seriously God's work and give their best to it.

We may hear how people have made sacrifices to follow Jesus. Actually, no one ever left anything for Jesus without being fully and completely rewarded many times and in many ways. We become more in this world by following Jesus than we could ever become without him.

I can recall when my children, Anna Marie and David were very young, and we were attempting to do something technically challenging. There was a little hesitation on all our parts, and then Anna Marie finally blurted out to her little brother, "David, you've got to get with it!" She couldn't have been more than seven or eight years-old, but she realized that if you're going to accomplish something you've got to commit to it and do it the right way. If we are to fulfill God's plan for our lives, we must "get with it" for God.

Hebrews 13:21 says,

"May He equip you with all you need for doing His will. May he produce in you, through the power of Jesus Christ, every good thing that is pleasing to Him. All glory to Him forever and ever! Amen"

In keeping with the spirited thought of "Getting with it for God" there are five things we must do to accomplish this:

Minimize your fears. Fear often paralyzes a person from trusting their God-given instincts. And even more, fear will quench the Spirit of God in our life if we let it. Our world is dangerous and violent. Crime fills our streets making them unsafe. But Christ is our safety. He watches over, protects, and keeps those who commit their lives to Him (John 6:20).

Maximize your faith. A Christian who lacks a working faith will disappoint themselves, discourage others, and defeat God's purposes. Prayer, effort, and a positive attitude naturally increase faith. And faith produces miracles, brings impossibilities to pass, and most of all, glorifies God (Mark 9:23).

Magnify your fervor. The people who are uninterested and unconcerned about the needs of others will find themselves to be indifferent. And if a Christian is this way, then they will surely be ineffective in their personal work for God. Romans 12:11 says,

"Never be lazy, be fervent, work hard, and serve the Lord enthusiastically."

To make a difference and have peace with what we have done, we must be fervent in service for God. Prayer and ardent zeal bring results when presenting Christ to the lost (James 5:16).

Manifest your freedom. Don't let doubts, unforgiveness, and resentments bind you from doing what God wants. These negative attributes will keep you from being the blessing you could be to the people who need you most. God will free us from the negative personalities that plague so many people today.

Mobilize your forces. Don't sit with folded hands anymore! Jesus said, "The harvest is plentiful, but the workers are few." Be a worker in God's field. We must be about the Master's business. The field is ripe unto harvest and its high time to witness and win the lost so that that they may know and experience God's love.

As Jesus grew from innocence to holiness, we too, can grow in grace and knowledge of our Lord as we commit ourselves to His work. We are not perfect like Christ, but we can grow into his likeness as we are busy for him in our trades, jobs, service, and personal witnessing. Let's always, wherever we are, be about our Father's business. To do so is to fulfill our own purpose for living!

How to Accomplish Things in Life

- Minimize your Fears.
- Maximize your Faith.
- Magnify your Fervor.
- Manifest your Freedom.
- Mobilize your Forces.

38

Making God the Priority

*"Seek the Kingdom of God above all else, and live righteously,
and He will give you everything you need"
(Matthew 6:33).*

There once was a young woman named Emma whose father died after a lengthy illness. He had worked hard all his life and passed on to her a good-sized inheritance. It helped put her through college and raise three young children. When she received the inheritance, she gave 10% of it to her church, believing this had been a blessing from God.

In another small town a man had been a faithful member of his local church and had religiously given his tithes and offerings to the church. When he died, it was discovered he had managed to save quite a lump sum of cash. In his will, he left his entire estate to the church. This investment helps the church pay most of its expenses related to the maintenance budget each year. In life and in death, he joyfully gave to God what had been given to him.

Little Allie gets an allowance from her parents. Each week she uses $10 for various expenses, puts $5 in the bank, puts $2 in the offering plate, and uses the other $3 for more candy than she needs, but nobody's perfect!

In 1 Samuel 1:26-28, Hannah testified,

"Many years ago, I prayed to the Lord and I asked Him to give me this boy, and He has granted my request. Now I am giving him to the Lord, and he will belong to the Lord his whole life."

When we give back to God from what God has given us, we are blessed beyond measure. Hannah's joy over the birth of Samuel, incredible as it was, was not complete. In God's own time, her joy was multiplied as she dedicated her son to God's service. Her faith inspires us to put God first and give back to Him what He has given us. When we do, He blesses us with all we need and more to share. Knowing this principle is true and worthy of our following, how do we go about giving God first place?

First, put Him before PLEASURE. We live in a pleasure-seeking world. Millions of dollars are spent on entertainment each year. Christians should be faithful and honest to worship God in church attendance, prayer, and the ministry of His Word before anything else (Matthew 6:33).

Second, put Him before POSITION. Some people make their job their top priority. And when inclement weather or company rolls in; a hindrance to church attendance is born. Jobs, responsibilities, and finances are necessary, but they should be kept in proper perspective.

Third, put Him before POPULARITY. It's very natural to want the approval of others. Even in school, youngsters want to be like the other kids. In the office or the factory, it's easy to go along with the crowd. However, gaining God's approval is most important. Christians should be on the offensive by giving witness for Him. By doing so, God assumes the responsibility of supplying us with courage and grace.

Fourth, put Him before POSSESSIONS. Luke 12:15 says,

> *"Beware! Guard against every kind of greed. Life is not measured by how much you own."*

The Bible also warns that the "love of money" is the root of all evil. God wants our wholehearted devotion. We should be faithful in paying God's tithes and giving offerings liberally as He blesses and meets our needs.

Finally, put Him before PEOPLE. No relationship is worth forsaking a faithful loving God who created you in the first place. Once I was downtrodden and depressed because a friend was no longer in my life. It was a burden that was getting too hard to carry and I shared my plight with another friend. He told me, "As much as you miss this person, understand that the ultimate fulfillment in relationships is found in Christ." It helped me turn the page and move on, because what he told me was the truth and I needed to be reminded of that.

Give God the first fruits of everything; the best you have to offer in every area of your life. When you feel weak in your commitment to this task, recall the words of Matthew 6:33, where it says,

"Seek the Kingdom of God (a relationship with Him) above all else, and live a life pleasing to God, and He will give you everything you need."

God as Priority in Life

- Before Pleasure.
- Before Position.
- Before Popularity.
- Before Possessions.
- Before People.

39

How to Live a Satisfying Life

"My purpose is to give them a rich and satisfying life"
(John 10:10).

The things of this world and our physical bodies are temporary and uncertain. Most of us are already taking medicine to patch up the holes in the temporary house in which we live. Despite all the patching we can do, our house (our body) will steadily grow old and become more and more uncomfortable. The troublesome things about our physical life is that peace often forsakes us before we die.

Clearly, based on God's Word, we can have peace in our heart and mind until the day we die. Jesus's own words announce this revelation:

"I am leaving you a gift, peace of mind and heart. And the peace I give is a gift the world cannot give. So, don't be troubled or afraid" (John 14:27).

The physical peace is what often disappears as we age; headaches, backaches, arthritis, failing eye sight and for many their hearing starts to wane. It's a wise person who will take care of themselves when they're young; for surely there will be payback one day on how well they have invested in healthy living. God intends for us to live a long good life. This is the ideal.

Deuteronomy 30:20 says,

"This is the key to your life. And if you love and obey the Lord, you will live long."

And again, in Ephesians 6:1-3,

"Do the right things, you will be well, and you will have a long life on the earth."

We all have a long race to run toward eternity. But here's the fatal mistake so many make. We want to place all our attention on the outward, physical life. We plan our financial future by working both day and night to lay up treasures to coddle ourselves into thinking that the physical life is the high life and nothing else deserves our attention or care.

A rich man was once showing a visiting preacher his grand house and vast outlay of land. He pointed in a northerly direction and said, "As far as the eye can see, that's all mine."

"Indeed!" said the minister.

Looking south and then west, he said, "That's all mine too. I have land at all four points of the compass."

"Yes, I see you have land on all four quarters, but," pointing his finger upward, "what have you in that direction?"

The man who was rich in possessions and the so-called good things of this physical life, realized that he was spiritually bankrupt. He blushed and stammered and had no answer.

The best thing about the imperishable inward person is that their beauty and all the needed strength may be renewed day by day. Spiritually we can be renewed as if it's the first day of our walk with God.

"God is faithful, and His mercies begin afresh each morning" (Lamentations 3:23).

Love, hope, and faith, the great abiding factors in this world, are capable of constant renewal. All three have their great source in God; Who is love, and Who keeps faith forever, and Who can inspire hope in us under all circumstances.

If we hungered for inward renewal as much as the physical, we would experience a glorious radiance that cannot be found in a cosmetic bottle or created through some vain surgical procedure. God sent an angel to feed

Elijah under the juniper tree in the desert when he was discouraged, worn-out, and in need of comfort (1 Kings 19). He will also provide strength to come back to us again when we need it. To keep the inward spirit of a person strong, they must have daily feeding. They must partake of regular meals and be renewed day by day. Some people go on religious sprees. They go to church regularly, hear sermons, but then drop away for long seasons of indifference. You can't be a healthy Christian living this way. We need not live such lives as this. We can renew our spiritual life day by day, so that our spiritual graces will be beautiful and helped inwardly seeing that we have spent time with God.

Just because the years pass and rob us of our youthful vigor, the spirit can be made new every day. An 80-year-old man once said, "My body and mind are weaker than they used to be, but my life grows richer everyday as I get into the higher altitudes of life."

If you are young in years, the wisest thing to do for your life is to pray to God each day in some private place. Then, having been inspired and comforted by your visit with the Holy Spirit, inhale the freshness of each new day and feel the exhilaration that comes as you start the race of life. But I can assure you, the sweetest hours of your days are when you near the sunset of your time on earth. As good as your physical life may be and as much as you may love life, there's nothing quite equal to the holy calm of a tired Christian pilgrim when at last they can see the hills and flowers of heaven. What a glorious thing to be able to grow old like that. To be happy, strong, and aspiring in old age we must begin in our youth to refresh and renew the inward spirit that is set apart for glory in the later years of life.

40

How God Calls Us

"God saves us and calls us to a holy life. Not because we deserved it, but because that was His plan from the beginning of time"
(2 Timothy 1:9).

A farmer was looking across his vast field one day and he was filled with love for how much God had blessed him. He lifted his eyes and hands to heaven and thanked God. As he peered into the skies he could see that the clouds had formed, what appeared to be the letters "GPC". He thought for a moment and concluded that the letters stood for "Go Preach Christ". He quickly called a deacon from his church and shared the news of this miraculous sign. The deacons of the church agreed to let him preach the following Sunday. The sermon was long, tedious, and very hard to understand. After the service, one of the deacons wistfully told the farmer, we have no doubt that you heard from God with the message in the sky, but we think God was telling you something else. Instead of telling you to "Go Preach Christ", He was telling you to "Go Plant Corn".

This would not be the first time a person was confused about their specific calling in life. It's the age-old question for all of us, "What on earth am I here for?" God told Jeremiah,

"Before I formed you in the womb I knew you; before you were born I set you apart; I appointed you as a prophet to the nations" (Jeremiah 1:5).

God has a purpose for each Christian. And whatever it is, it should be done for the glory of God (1 Corinthians 10:31).

God calls people of diverse backgrounds and vocations to represent Him in the world. When Jesus called his twelve disciples, he didn't draft them, force them, or ask them to volunteer; he chose them to serve him in special ways. He doesn't twist our arms and make us do something we simply don't want to do. Christ calls today and we either accept him and join Him, or we reject Him and set out to find ourselves. Jesus called people of all walks of life—fisherman, tax collectors, political activists, and doctors. He called the rich and poor; educated and uneducated. You don't have to fit a certain mold to be used by God. He can use anyone, no matter how insignificant he or she appears.

I believe there are 5 distinct calls that we all must decide to answer or not.

First, there's the "Call to Salvation". Christ's call to salvation goes out to everyone. Salvation is received by repentance and faith. A godly sorrow for sins, accompanied by faith, brings victory through Jesus Christ. 1 Timothy says,

"Fight the good fight of faith. Take hold of the eternal life to which you were called when you made your good confession in the presence of many witnesses."

Secondly, there's the "Call to Sacrifice". We must deny ourselves if we expect to positively affect the lives of others. We win by going out, reaching out, and giving our time, talent, and treasure.

Third, we're all "Called to Suffer". Yes, some suffer more than others, but it doesn't mean that God is playing favorites. We need to recognize the purpose in suffering. It teaches lessons, tests faith, testifies to others, and trains for service. 1 Peter 2:21 says,

"To this you were called, because Christ suffered for you, leaving you an example, that you should follow in his steps".

Fourth, there's the "Call to Separation". As a child of God, you have been set apart for good works, even in the face of hardships. Even though real estate, automobiles, stocks, and other possessions have captured our devotion, to accept this call we must set our affections on things above (Colossians 3:2). Are you being set apart by love, faith, prayer, Bible reading, faithful church attendance, and stewardship?

Finally, there's the "Call to Service". Selfish excuses and a lack of concern hinders many Christians from heeding God's call to service. If you haven't discovered God's specific call or assignment just yet, then seek to fulfill the mission common to all believers—love everyone, obey God, and help others when you can. Do these things until His guidance becomes clearer. God understands our confusion about the future because we simply don't know what's in store. But He has given us an insight into what is waiting for us:

"I pray that your heart will be flooded with light so that you can understand the confident hope He has given to those He called—His holy people who are His rich and glorious inheritance" (Ephesians 1:18).

Your future is bright with opportunity! Seek God with all your heart and watch His plan unfold for you.

<u>God's Specific Calls</u>

- ♦ Call to Salvation.

- ♦ Call to Sacrifice.

- ♦ Called to Suffer.

- ♦ Call to Separation.

- ♦ Call to Service.

41

How to Renew Your Life

"Anyone who commits their life to the Lord, becomes a new person. The old life is gone; a new life has begun!"
(2 Corinthians 5:17).

The greatest spirituality in a person can never be attained when pursuing the things of the world. A person left alone will not know the joys of abundant living because worldliness suffocates the soul. The "high life" requires a rigorous climb up the mountainside. When a person chooses the road less traveled—the one that rises above all others, there are mountains of spiritual heights on which to roam. These are the people who give themselves up to the higher things. They are the "go-getters", the aspiring personalities, those who don't settle. They seek, out of pure spiritual adrenaline, the abundant life Jesus Christ came to give to all.

On a trip to the Blue Ridge Mountains, I took advantage of the scenic beauty and trekked up the hillside. The further I hiked the more inspired I became. I was far removed, or though it seemed, from the domestic stresses of work and all that's associated with deadlines and reports. It's understandable why Christ often escaped into the mountains (Matthew 19:23). I began to see and experience God's glory and what it means to live on the "high lands" of the soul. I felt a renewed energy enter my body. In the mountains not only is the air purer, but I discovered, symbolically, God feeds the mountain climber on honey that's hidden among the rocks (Psalm 81:16). He shares with the seeking soul what He knows they need. There's also a window of confession and a purification of your heart. To waste it or to turn away from the open window is to forsake what's for your own good. When we declare that we're dead to our own selfishness, Christ in turn makes our spirit come alive. This presence of Christ in our hearts, gives us the feeling that what we're doing; we do for him and it makes all our work greater and nobler.

I left the trails that day renewed and ready to "get with it" for God. Let's be reminded of Hebrews 13:21:

"May He equip you with all you need for doing His will. May He produce in you through the power of Jesus Christ, every good thing that is pleasing to Him. All glory to Him forever and ever! Amen."

There are five methods to help an encouraged heart to become an ambassador for Christ.

First, you minimize your fears. Our world is full of dangers. Violence and crime fill our streets, making them unsafe by day and night. Christ provides us a safety zone within himself. Claim his words of promise from Mark 6:50:

"Don't be afraid. Take courage! I am here."

He watches over, protects, and keeps those who commit their lives to him.

Next, you must maximize your faith. Even Christians can be guilty of a lacking-faith. The devil robs us when we yield to his seductions. We're all guilty of disappointing ourselves, discouraging others, and defeating God's purposes. But we can increase our faith through prayer, effort, and a positive attitude. Faith is the key that unlocks miracles and brings impossibilities to pass. These are the things that glorify God.

Third, an inspired person will magnify their favor. It's remarkable, but some Christians are uninterested and unconcerned about the needs of others. And because they're indifferent, they're ineffective. Don't let this characterize your actions. We must be fervent in our service for God. Being partnered in prayer with an ardent group of believers brings results when presenting Christ to the lost. Romans 12:11 says,

"Never be lazy, work hard, and serve the Lord
enthusiastically."

A motivated Christian will manifest their freedom. It's true that doubt and resentment come to all of us and many people become bound by them. When this happens they're unable to be the blessings they should be. Being aware of your God-given freedoms can enable Christ to free us from selfishness, resentment, hatred, and strife.

Finally, perhaps the greatest thing a Christian can do to be a Kingdom multiplier is to mobilize their forces. Jesus announced,

"The harvest is great, but the workers are few"
(Matthew 9:37).

To make a difference in our lives and those around us we must be about the Master's business. The field is ripe and ready to be harvested. It's high time to witness to others about what God is doing in our lives. These conversations can win the lost and help them raise their level of living.

Some people need a lifeline in the form of encouragement that will help them scale the heights to a higher place in life. Mountains are made to climb, and a Christian has all they need in Christ to make their way to the top. Christ has been to the mountain and has experience in climbing them. Therefore, let him be your trail guide through the maze of turmoil and misdirection the world throws at you.

42

Share to Show You Care

"Be rich in good works and generous to those in need, always be ready to share with others. By doing this, you will be storing up treasures as a good foundation for the future so that they may experience true life"
(1 Timothy 6:18).

Despite our differences, we were made for human fellowship. While some personalities are quite content on keeping to themselves, generally, we are starved and stunted in every way when we live selfish lives. Nobody is so poor within themselves than the person who shuts their sympathies away from their counterparts and devotes themselves entirely to looking out for number one (aka: self).

After a brief conversation about helping others and giving when the opportunity affords itself, my daughter laughingly quipped, "Sharing is caring!" And she's right. It's just as sure as the law of gravitation that if we divide with others God's good gifts to us, we multiply instead of diminishing our blessings.

A wonderful illustration of giving and being blessed is found in 1 Kings 17:7-24. A widow gives some water and bread to a hungry and thirsty Elijah. As a result of her giving, God blessed her with an abundance of food. The Bible goes on to say that the widow's son becomes sick and Elijah helped save him from death. This old story reveals a law of God also found in 2 Corinthians 9:7-8 that can't be changed:

"You must each decide in your heart how much to give. And don't give reluctantly or in response to pressure. God loves a person who gives cheerfully. And God will generously provide all you need. Then you will always have everything you need, and plenty left over to share with others".

The way to be blessed is to give to others. In other words, when you're blessed by something, find a creative and genuine way to give a little of that blessing away to someone else. By doing this you keep the cycle of God's blessings flowing in and through you. Unselfishness is an invulnerable and bulletproof piece of armor in any world which belongs to God.

In the Roman Army there was a law that no one should approach the Emperor's tent at night or they would be subject to the death penalty. One night a soldier was found near the royal tent, bearing a petition he wished to present. He was sentenced to death at once. Upon hearing the voices, the Emperor asked what the trouble was. Finding out the soldier had entered the forbidden ground, he gave this command: "If the petition be for himself, let him die, but if it's for another, spare his life." The soldier's plea was for two fellow soldiers who had fallen asleep at their posts. The pleading soldier's life was spared.

God is still more gracious, for when we come to Him in prayer on behalf of others He will also hear our requests for ourselves. It was when Job, of the Old Testament, forgetting his own great losses and troubles, sought God on behalf of his friends. God brought joy again into Job's heart and life.

By sharing what we have with others we give a practical exhibition of our trust and confidence in God. We show we're not afraid to trust God to give us more blessings. We often pray God do for others what He has already given us the means to do in His name. Real prayer, the kind that moves mountains, requires us to actively be cultivating our relationship with God. Why pray something for someone when you already have the abundant means to relieve your neighbor's distress and yet will not do it? Why pray about the conversion of your friend when you're unwilling to speak with them about your own personal testimony and the knowledge of God's great love? Many pray for God to save sinners, many well-intentioned people pray for an outpouring of the Holy

Spirit in the church services, many pray for pastors to start revivals, but week after week we share nothing of Christ with anyone outside the church walls!

Let's each of us co-operate with God and look for opportunities to witness of what God has done, is doing, and will do in our lives. Look for ways to share the hope of Christ, encourage with words and smiles, and we will see the wonderful days of salvation. Remember, sharing is caring! Share what spiritual blessings God has already given you with unbelieving friends, neighbors, and family and you will find that you lack no good thing.

43

Appealing to Heaven Through Prayer

"Search for the Lord and for His strength; continually seek Him. Remember the wonders He has performed, His miracles, and the rulings He has given"
(1 Chronicles 16:11-12).

There was a flag used in the darkest hours of the Revolutionary War. It was called the Tree Flag (or Appeal to Heaven Flag). It wasn't the stars and stripes. It wasn't red, white, and blue. Gen. George Washington unfurled a simple white flag with an evergreen tree sewn on it. Above the tree were the words: "APPEAL TO HEAVEN". As commander in chief of the Continental Army, Washington knew that he was out-gunned, out-manned, and didn't have near the supplies when compared with the mighty British Army. The flag represented Washington's prayers as they forged their way through Virginia. He knew that without an intervention of God, this new nation would die before it ever had a chance to stand on its own.

The words on the flag were an expression from a treatise written by the English philosopher John Locke. In that treatise, Locke asserted that when people have exhausted all courts, arbitrators, and kings, "then they may appeal to Heaven". Many historians fail to give emphasis to the well-documented fact that the Revolutionary War was accompanied by a strong wave of prayer. The green and white flag symbolized this revival of prayer—a sign of the godly desperation and appeal of our founding fathers to our heavenly Father.

Hardly a day goes by that we don't have some controversy and violence in our nation. Therefore, it's high time to appeal to heaven. We need this resource more than anything else. Prayer is a mighty force. God does things in answer to prayer that He would not do otherwise.

I can quickly recall seven biblical men of faith that appealed to Heaven:

Abraham prayed with **COMMITMENT**. Abraham's faith had been severely tested. When he prayed with commitment to the will of God, God intervened. Genesis 22:11 says,

"The Angel of the Lord called to him from heaven, Abraham! Abraham! Yes, Abraham replied, here I am!"

When we commit our will totally to God's will, our prayers will prevail also.

Jacob prayed without ***CONSTRAINT***. God told Jacob to return home, but he feared Esau. Jacob prayed with persistence and God answered. The Bible said,

"He wrestled with God and man; and prevailed"
(Genesis 32:28).

We must also lift our hands toward heaven and touch God without constraint. God will answer when we prevail in prayer for ourselves and others.

Moses prayed with ***CONCERN***. Because the Israelites made idols, God threatened to destroy them. Moses intervened by putting his life on the line for them. God will hear and answer the intervening prayer of concern we have for unconverted friends, loved ones, and those under the heavy burden of guilt and shame.

David prayed with ***CONTRITION***. "Have mercy on me, Oh God, because of your unfailing love; blot out the stains of my sins." When David repented of his sin with humility and contrition, God forgave and restored to him the joy of salvation. Our prayers, also, must come from a humble and contrite heart. God will forgive us; His mercy endures forever!

Elijah prayed with ***CONFIDENCE***. He prayed with faith to the true, living God (1 Kings 18:37-38). The fire fell, the rain came, and the skeptics believed. Elijah's God answered prayer. The prayer of faith will move mountains and will move God's hand to forgive and cleanse us. He is the same miracle-working God who changes not.

Daniel prayed with **COURAGE**. Daniel didn't buckle under threat. God honored his courageous devotion and faith and protected him from the lions. Daniel 6:10 says,

"Daniel, at home, knelt down and prayed before God; giving thanks".

In the face of persecution, our prayers of courageous faith also will be heard by God, who can deliver us as He did Daniel.

Jesus prayed with **COMPASSION**. In Jesus' darkest hour and most excruciating hour, he prayed with compassion for those who despitefully use us. We too can grow and learn to love them because God first loved us.

Our appeals to heaven through prayer need not be a last resort, but the first resort! More than schools, armies, jobs, or healthcare, we need a viable, daily prayer life. Prayer is the Christian's life line. God tells us how to be made whole as an individual and a nation when he says,

"If my people who are called by My name will humble themselves and pray and seek My face and turn from their wicked ways, I will hear from heaven and will forgive their sins and restore their land. My ears will be attentive to every prayer" (2 Chronicles 7:14-15).

We need to appeal to heaven for our families, relationships, and churches. When we pray, we enter a covenant with Jesus, and his promise: If we ask it will surely be given to us and will benefit us and our relationship with him.

How We Should Pray

- With Commitment.
- With Constraint.
- With Concern.
- With Contrition.
- With Confidence.
- With Courage.
- With Compassion.

44

Living With Consequences and Hope for the Future

*"Your Word is a lamp to guide my feet and a light for my path.
My life hangs in the balance I will not stop obeying Your
instructions"
(Psalm 119:105, 109).*

There once was a religious and political leader who lived in the Caucasus Mountains. He led his people through a long war against Russia trying to maintain their independence. He knew for his people to be at their strongest all wrongdoing needed to be rooted out. He decreed a sentence of 100 lashes for such things as bribery and forgery. The first person brought to him was his own mother. She was found guilty of her crimes based on witness and testimony. He locked himself up for a day of prayer. When he finally came out he announced the punishment must be inflicted. After five lashes had been administered to his mother, he jumped up and shouted,

"Halt!" He took the final ninety-five lashes on his own back. There's a price that must be paid for sin and there's a price that must be paid for crime.

I worked in a state correctional facility for almost 15 years. This arm of law enforcement has the task of making sure the penalty of breaking the law is carried out. Few people have gone through the experience of committing a crime and then being forgiven for it. When a criminal serves out their sentence they may legally be restored to society, but some continue to bear their guilt in their own mind. Like sin in our life, some of our so-called friends and those we commit a crime against may never forgive. This makes it difficult to forgive ourselves.

However, every person has committed crimes against God. Not a single human being has kept God's commandments perfectly. Every person is judged guilty because of their sins. It may seem to us from outward appearances that law-breakers against the Lord go free. God doesn't hold a Divine law court in which we are arrested by angels, charged of sin, and pronounced guilty by a cloud of witnesses. Even though we don't see God carrying out this process we know in our hearts what it means to be guilty of sin. We feel the burden this places on our minds. This is because God's Holy Spirit convicts us. God's conviction is not enjoyable, but it is necessary to keep ourselves in check with Him. God loves us and makes it possible to be right with Him. Part of His work is to judge people because of their lack of conformity to His righteousness. John 16:8-11 says, "When the Holy Spirit comes, He will show the world the truth about sin. He will show the world about being right with God. And He will show the world what it is to be guilty because the leader of this world (Satan) is guilty".

God's conviction should be seen as one way God protects people from dangerous and poor decision-making. We have been warned that one day God will exact eternal judgement on every guilty sinner who has not repented and asked for forgiveness. The Christian, who has welcomed Jesus Christ into their heart as their Savior, is free from guilt and the burden of sin. A Christian doesn't have to live with the torment of judgement upon them. The weight of wrong-doing has been removed. Chris died for you so you wouldn't have to pay the penalty of sinful choices. He was and is your substitute. The Christian knows what it's like to be guilty of crimes against God and to be forgiven of those crimes. Every one of us, regardless of our background can unload our burden of sin on the Savior. We can live with an attitude of gratitude for what Christ has done for us. May we all seek to help someone else find freedom and release from the load of a guilty conscience. You don't have to live day-to-day carrying guilt about your sins from the past.

Every person has gone astray and got lost. It's because they've "turned their own way". We all have a choice to make: will it be our way or God's? We reason in our mind that the human-centered way is best, and that God is outdated for our technological age. Proverbs 14:12 says,

"There is a way which looks right to a person, but its end is the way of death."

Jesus' own words are:

"I am the Way and the Truth and the Life. No one can go to the Father except by me" (John 14:6).

Left to ourselves we are lost and wondering. We have our own desires and pleasures that do not last, and we seek the next thrill to pursue. Do not be a sheep without a shepherd. Choose not to plunge headlong toward a destructive and unsure future. But choose Christ and let him put the pieces back together. In Christ you will find the way to life. You must take the step of faith and turn toward Christ. If you will do that, as your Shepherd, he will feed, sustain, and lead you into green pastures as a trustworthy guardian. He will be your guide and give you direction. This is God's promise and His wonderful provision for our waywardness.

45

A Family Pet Gives a Divine Message

"Remember that the Lord will give you an inheritance as your reward, and that the Master you are serving is Christ"
(Colossians 3:24).

On Christmas Eve in 2004, I traveled to a nearby town with my children and my father to meet a man and his wife who bred Labrador Retrievers. The meeting had been prearranged and we looked forward to this new addition to our family. The little 8-week-old black lab took turns being cuddled in the laps of both Anna Marie and David on the drive back. The dog was really my Dads, but we all claimed him as part of the family unit.

As is with most Labs, they generally don't live past 10-12 years. Sport, as we called him, lived to be 14. I pause to reflect on the lessons we learned from him and I can point to very specific examples of character traits he possessed; kindness, endurance, obedience, and brotherly love, just to name a few. All of which are traits encouraged by the Divine Word.

As my Dad was the primary caregiver and spent most of the time with him, he invariably became Sport's master. I saw this with my own eyes. My Dad likes sharing the story that Sport would often back away from his food bowl when the long-haired tabby cat came in for a taste test. It always baffled me that a grown dog would give up his meal (usually only a few morsels) to a cat. But he did. It was kindness in character that he did so. He would back away and look at his master as if to say, "OK, I'll let him eat first."

When Sport was 18 months old, he ran 7 miles with me through sand, hills, and creeks; never once asking me to stop and quit. He had endurance that made him strong physically.

Sometimes, when visiting my parents, while Sport roamed the nearby country side, I could call him three or four times before he'd acknowledge me. But when by Dad called him, it took one time and here he'd come. He exercised obedience to the master.

I once adopted a German Shepherd because we felt Sport might like a buddy. He welcomed him into his dog yard with no hesitation. They enjoyed a brief friendship until lightning struck and killed his friend. But it wasn't before Sport shared some brotherly love with a fellow canine. Sport's life was the envy of every dog that lives the country life.

On his last day, in an old and feeble state, we loaded him into his carrier for what was to be his final trip to the Vet. I purposefully looked into his eyes. Though his hearing had diminished, his eyesight was still good, and he was fixed on his master, my Dad. I reached in to pet him one last time, he acknowledged it by lowering his head, but he kept his eye on his master. His master had provided for him, took care of him, gave him shelter from the storms, shared many memorable days running through the fields and trails around home. Sport was most content when in the company of his master and leisurely spending time with him. He trusted his master, even when his health was failing and he barely had strength enough to stand, he kept his eye on his master.

These illustrations beg the question, are you looking to the Master, which is Jesus Christ? Hebrews 12:1-2 says,

"Let us run with endurance the race God has set before us. We do this by keeping our eyes on Jesus (the Master), the champion who initiates and perfects our faith".

We must run our race all the way to the end, fixing our eyes on Jesus, the Master.

We need to Look to the Master *IN* everything. Many people are ready to look to Jesus when trouble strikes, but when everything is going well; they lean on their own limited strength and fail. We must look to Jesus in every-thing—in good times as well as bad, in joy as well as sor-row, and in triumph as well as trial. The Scripture admon-ishes us to:

"Look to Jesus that we may obtain mercy and we will find grace to help us when we need it most" (Hebrews 4:16).

We also need to Look to the Master ***FOR*** everything. Some do not depend on the Lord to supply all their needs. They rely on self-effort and other people and sooner or later experience disappointment. We should look to Jesus for life, love, food, clothing, and shelter. We are promised ample supply for all our needs:

"God, who takes care of me, will supply all your needs from his glorious riches, which have been given to us in Christ Je-sus (the Master)" (Philippians 4:19).

We need to Look to the Master ***WITH*** everything. To reap the benefits of God's care, we mustn't reserve por-tions of our life from Him. He can be trusted. If we're to be victorious, we must look to Jesus (the Master) with everything—time, talent, and treasure. We must be totally dedicated to him (Romans 12:1).

Finally, we need to Look to the Master ***THROUGH*** everything. Look to Christ more than just in the good times. And don't blame him when suffering and tragedy strikes. God often allows suffering to strengthen our faith and fulfill his purpose. We must continue to look to Jesus (the Master) and seek his purpose with patience and trust.

Sport, the 14-year-old black lab finished his race and kept his eye on his master all the way to the end. Are you looking to the Master, Jesus Christ, just now in your present circumstances? Trust in God to help you live the life he has given you. No matter how long your race in life, keep on running, and finish the race with your eyes on the Master.

46

God's Protection Can Lead to Second Chances

"Jesus asked where are your accusers? I do not condemn you.
Go and sin no more."
(John 8:10-11).

Have you ever longed to start over because you made mistakes that caused yourself and others heartache and trouble? Sometimes it takes mistakes in life to get our attention. I've known people who exhausted all human strength before acknowledging their helplessness. It's at this point in life that you have your greatest potential, for if you truly have reached rock-bottom, there's nowhere else to go, but up! God stands ready and available to help the poorest and most desolate soul in need. The most wonderful prospect is that the greatest power source in all creation is available to the small and to the mighty. It makes no difference how popular you are or how much money or talent you have. God's powerful touch is available to all that will call upon his name.

I once met a man at a function our church had coordinated. He began to tell me about his life. He grew up in a home where he lacked for no material thing. In fact, he had more than most. As he grew into adulthood he began to drink beer and other strong drinks regularly. He would often function in a drunken stupor. Friends and family would warn him that he needed help and his addiction was going to consume his life. He would always dismiss their warnings and he'd continue to reach for the bottle. One day he started drinking around noon and continued into the night and eventually got behind the wheel and started to drive. He came to his senses after a police chase. He lived in Florida but found himself staring into the gun chamber of a state trooper's revolver on some unknown highway in Nebraska! He had no idea how he had driven that far. The officer drug him out of his car and said, "Make one move and you're dead!"

Later that same evening while staring at the ceiling in a jail cell, he told himself. "Maybe I do have a drinking problem." His mind reverted back to the wholesome upbringing he had enjoyed. Then, he decided to pray: "Lord I really messed up my life with my drinking. Will you forgive me? Will you touch my life with your healing hands and please take away my desire for alcohol? I want to do better at living, please help me." From that day on, he never drank another drop.

Three things were at work in this man's life—the desire to make a change, the power of prayer to make it happen, and God's providential care for human life. My mentor, Norman Vincent Peale once said, "Decisions can be made in prayer if you stick to it. Don't mumble a few prayers and expect that to do it. You've got to stay with it and wrestle with the Lord".

I believe when a person desires to be divinely touched by God's miracle-working hand people can be changed instantly. There's a specific verse in the Bible that says,

"There went with him a group of men whose hearts God had touched" (1 Samuel 10:26).

The need of individuals, homes, schools, churches, nations, and the world is the touch of the Master's hand. Christ is waiting to touch all who will receive and trust him.

Scripture tells of a man who desired to be healed.

"Lord, the man said, if you're willing, you can heal me and make me clean. Jesus reached out and touched him. I am willing, Jesus said. Be healed! Instantly he was healed and made clean" (Matthew 8:3).

God's touch is "CLEANSING" for those who pray for it. When Christians make a total commitment of their life to God, the Holy Spirit cleanses them with God's love.

God's cleansing empowers, enables, and encourages people for service. Envy, strife and resentment are washed away (1 John 1:7).

For those that desire it, God's touch is also "CONVERTING". It brings forgiveness when we confess, repent, and believe we receive his pardon. It's a touch that transforms us. Old things pass away, and everything becomes new—new life, hope, purpose, goals, and destiny (2 Corinthians 5:17). Christ's converting touch brings a release from guilt and we're set free from the bondage of sin that we allow to control us.

All of us become perplexed about problems, we're fearful of future things, and troubled at the thought of death. Matthew 17:7 says,

"Jesus came over and touched them and he said, get up and don't be afraid."

God's touch is a "COMFORTING" touch.

The Master's touch gives life. Therefore, it's a "CONQUERING" touch. It enables us to see, hear, feel, and know we're alive in Christ! His touch brings physical, mental, and spiritual healing to those who believe.

If you don't like where you've allowed your life to wander; if you want to start over and try again, you can! God says,

"I am about to do something new. Look! I've already begun!

Do you not see it? I will make a pathway in the wilderness. I will create rivers in the dry waste land" (Isaiah 43:19).

This is the Divine motivation that you've been waiting for and needing to hear. Embrace it in all its fullness! And remember, God's touch is cleansing, converting, comforting, and conquering. Choose this day to allow God to change you from the inside out. And start living with the purpose God intended for you.

The Traits of God's Touch

It is Cleansing.

It is Converting.

It is Comforting.

It is Conquering.

47

Take the High Road When Being Criticized

"Bless those who persecute you. Don't curse them. Pray for them"
(Romans 12:14).

A friend of mine contacted me and commenced to unload her pent-up emotions and feelings about how she was treated at work. She was feeling defeated, dejected, and was spiraling into the darkness of pain and despair.

"It's so unfair!" she said, "To have things said about me that are untrue is really hurtful. I try to treat people right and mind my own business, but people have it out to get me. Sometimes I think it's not worth the trouble of trying to do the right thing."

"If you know who's spreading the gossip, have you tried talking to them? Maybe you could talk to your supervisor if it's affecting your work performance," I suggested.

"I know who it is, and I've talked to my boss and they tell me there's nothing they can do because it's hearsay. So, I'm stuck dealing with being talked down to and disrespected."

As she talked, the Spirit reminded me of a Scripture passage found in Luke 6:28:

"Bless those who curse you. Pray for those who hurt you."

I explained to her this scenario happens all too often to people, especially those who are honestly seeking to live a Christian life. The devil orchestrates the plan to use people and circumstances to discourage our faith. Some people put others down because of jealously, insecurities, and other selfish reasons. During these times we must remind ourselves of the gospel. We must talk to our soul. Much like the psalmist did in Psalm 42:5-6,

"Why am I discouraged? Why is my heart so sad? I will put my hope in God! I will praise Him again—my Savior and my God!"

The writer of Psalm was upset about the loss of God's presence and his mistreatment at the hands of enemies. And he found himself in a place where his soul was very troubled, and where the only medicine strong enough was the truth. He needed to be reminded that God was his faithful Savior, so he preached this truth to his own heart.

We need to speak to our hearts because we need to hear

the truth of the gospel every day. We are weak, and life is tough. God loves us and we need to remind ourselves we're not alone in our troubles when we call upon God. God's presence and His love are not based on what a person has said about you at your workplace. God's love is based on what His Son Christ has done for you. Be of good cheer! Talk to your own soul. Encourage yourself with God's love.

When someone hurts you with lies, untruth, or treats you with disrespect, do not try to get even, take the high road and do the following:

CONSIDER THE SOURCE. Some hurt others because of ignorance or frustration, or possibly from some unfortunate experience in their past. Others deliberately and maliciously injure others because of satanic dominion in their lives. Consider your source—God is the Christian's fount of strength. Understanding and compassion will often heal your hurt. Pray earnestly for and forgive your offender.

CONSIDER THE SPIRIT. Many hurt others unintentionally, unaware of the impact of their words or actions. Contrarily, some try to lift self-esteem by putting others down, or hurt others to get even. Consider your Spirit—always give others the benefit of the doubt. If someone hurts you without intent and awareness, then quickly forgive and try to forget. If the injury was deliberate, pray for your offender. Forgive them. Love them; despite it. It's the only true way to overcome it without it overcoming you with bitterness and resentment. Remember it's their problem; don't make it yours. Keep a good spirit—God's Holy Spirit. Remember, also, the words of 1 Peter 4:14:

"So be happy when you are insulted for being a Christian, for then the glorious Spirit of God rests upon you."

CONSIDER THE SOLACE. There is no solace from God for those who deliberately and maliciously injure His children. God will make recompense. Consider your solace.

"God is our refuge and strength, a very present help in times of trouble" (Psalm 46:1).

Continue to love, forgive, and pray for those who despitefully use you. God is your solace, and you are more than a conqueror through Him.

Validate the fact you are a Child of God by repeatedly telling yourself that you are. Say, "I'm a Child of God. I'm a Child of God—fearfully and wonderfully made!" And for this reason, you can overcome anything the devil seems to throw at you. Evil would not want anything better than for you to cower in self-pity or lash out in anger. You are better than that! Choose to possess a bigger heart and one with an extra dose of courage. Consider the source, consider the Spirit, and consider the solace. Pray

for yourself that your soul would find hope and rest in God, not dejection and turmoil in circumstances.

<u>How to Take the High Road When Criticized</u>

- ♦ Consider the Source.
- ♦ Consider the Spirit.
- ♦ Consider the Solace.

48

Be Enthusiastic About Helping Others

"Don't be selfish. Don't look out only for your own interests, but take an interest in others, too"
(Philippians 2:3-4).

I think the only life that can possibly have enough power to give fresh impulse to others with sustainability, is one that has a positive nature and is confidently assertive. It mustn't only be good, but it must be vitally and positively good. It must be active and alive and have a conquering quality that will win the imagination and hopeful desire of others. But is this possible with Christianity when so many see the Christian life as one of "don't do this" and "don't do that"?

I believe there is too much emphasis put on what we give up for Christ. People tend to think that becoming a Christian means that the "fun life of adventure and good times" are all over. It seems to me when we turn the whole matter around and look at the other side of it, we can ask, "What can I do that will best show my love for Christ?" There's no virtue in giving up things. Anyone can do that! But only a Christian can approach life with devotion and enthusiasm and wear it with such love and fidelity that it becomes beautiful and attractive to those that see it in action. It's not enough that we're true and honest. We must be beautifully true and graciously honest. Christ urges us to live so attractively that we show others what they're missing by not being Christian. Being a Christian is not about losing or giving things up but gaining and obtaining the loving favor of God.

In a world that glorifies self-expression, how many times do we see good, purposeful gifts displayed with egotism, so they lose their best influences. We need to share our life experiences but keep the right spirit about us.

When people try to out give one another in the public arena there's a tendency for it to discourage other people from giving. Either they think what they have to offer is not good enough or would not make a difference when compared to someone else's. Its purity, motivation, and simplicity that makes giving beautiful.

A wonderful verse that clearly dictates the proper stewardship of giving is found in Romans 12:8,

"If your gift is to encourage others, be encouraging. If it is

*giving, give generously. If God has given you leadership abil-
ity, take the responsibility seriously. And if you have a gift for
showing kindness to others, do it gladly."*

In the case of the 10 lepers (Luke 17:11-19), all of
them were healed, but only one of them came back to
give thanks to Jesus. Jesus asked, "Where are the other
nine?" I don't doubt the other nine were thankful and they
did have enough faith to be healed, but they lacked the
beautiful spirit of praise and thanksgiving. Many people
are living the same way today. They believe God, Jesus,
the Holy Spirit, and they live prayerfully honorable lives.
But they don't make their lives more attractive with the
constant spirit of thanksgiving in every circumstance—in
business, social life, and in the home. It's only by completely surrendering our lives in devotion to Christ that
the attractive graces of the spirit provoke others to personal accountability.

Living a life in this way renders our service to Christ
for eternal gains. I believe that duty to a cause will
strengthen passion. It takes both to accomplish anything
worthy and noble in life. There's no passion without its
duty and no duty without its passion. To truly love Christ
and have passion for him is to want to perform our duties
in respect to his divine commands. When a person accepts
Christ's offer of salvation, they become a new person,

"The old life is gone; a new life has begun"
(2 Corinthians 5:17).

The new impulse to love like Christ loves descends upon us with a freshness so strong that our soul fills with pity when a need comes knocking at our door. God will give you courage to help the oppressed and the neglected will be attracted to you for protection, counsel, and help. This strange occurrence happens because God gives you light and the clouds that have darkened the lives of others will draw them to you. Let's all find our place in Christ and God will give us Christ's work to do in our day and time. God will not allow your work done in His Spirit to be lost or in vain.

49

Bring Beauty to Life

"Do not withhold good when it's in your power to help"
(Proverbs 3:27).

Many years ago, there was a man who had a farm on the outskirts of a very small community in the country. He took great pride in making his acreage as attractive as he possibly could. He would drive in search of some flower, tree, or shrub he didn't have growing at his farm, and he would transplant them on some favorable spot. Then one day he realized he had been thinking only of himself, so he started doing the same thing, but transplanted them on and around the grounds of his church. He continued this practice until he died. By the time he passed on, he had increased the flora of his native community by over a hundred varieties. What had once been a barren area, the church grounds became the most beautiful spot in the community.   The special significance of the story of this man lies in the fact that he started looking beyond his own desires and considered how he could make his community better, naturally. There's plenty of people who are greedy to enjoy beautiful things just for themselves. This man took the whole neighborhood into his view and labored to make the entire community a delightfully beautiful place to live and worship.

Is there not a message in this for us in our relationship to the Christian church? There needs to be more emphasis on the necessity of making the church attractive in order that it be affective in winning people to Christ and encouraging the faith of other Christians. In the little country church where I serve, we are small, but mighty in Spirit. The members do a fine job in organizing and making special events attractive where people from different churches throughout the community come together.

Understanding the story, I shared, wouldn't the church be an attractive light in the community for a new family that sees the neighborhood as a beautiful place in which to live? The same principle works in relation to the church. If the church is attractive because of its spiritual graces and because love is cultivated not only those who aren't Christians will be attracted to it, but it will have the power to fascinate those who are already settled members in it. This power of love can bless the existing members, strengthen them, and barring a surrender to temptation, keep their devotion.

A good question for each of us to ask ourselves is, "What can I do to make the church more beautiful?"

There are several things a person can do to add beauty and blessing to the church houses.

First, you can be good. The power of simple goodness can never be over emphasized.

Second, you can practice brotherly kindness or be a good neighbor, we all have social needs. To attempt to shut ourselves out from the world is to stunt the growth of our own better nature. Where there's activity and more things to do, worldly temptations are greater. Where there's less things and the simple life is before you, a more wholesome disposition can be better cultivated. Genuine friendship within the church can help the lonely and the stressed to blossom into a wonderful fragrance, which in turn adds to the beauty of the church.

Another thing we can do is to be cheerful. There's no place where cheerfulness is at a higher premium than in the church. People come to church usually after a hard week of toil and struggle. Many times, we go to church weary and bruised in our hearts and our spirits. Speaking a word of encouragement meets people in that condition. They need it even though they may not know it. A kind word, hearty handshake, or big hug can help the discouraged heart and make life worth living again.

Still another thing that makes the church beautiful is the worship experience. Nothing so exalts a church family as genuine church family worship. It brings all the dignity and glory of the Lord right at the footsteps of every member. It causes us to forget about ourselves and our differences. In a majestic way it illuminates the very thing that brings us together, which is love. What wonder we possess because Christ came down from Heaven, emptied himself of all glory. Being born into our likeness, yet he gave his life as a ransom for us all. Christ said,

"There is no greater love than to lay down one's life for one's friends" (John 15:13).

The church is most beautiful when it celebrates what Christ has done and continues to do for all who trust him. God has commended his love to us, because while we were sinners, Christ died for us. Now, he lives for us and intercedes on our behalf when we pray. Let's all seek to find what we can do to add to the church's power of love and beauty. We magnify God's love and our own capacity to love by voicing it in prayer and praise. Thank God for the privilege of life, liberty, and love.

<u>How to Bring Beauty to a Church</u>

- ♦ Be good.
- ♦ Be kind.
- ♦ Be cheerful.
- ♦ Be worshipful.

50

Finding the Way to Heaven

*"Jesus told them, I am the way, the truth, and the life. No one
can come to the Father except through me"
(John 14:6).*

There's a true story about an army combat unit that
was holding the line in the trench of a heated battle. They
came under very heavy fire. Pieces of shrapnel were
whizzing past all the Soldiers. Suddenly, one of them
took a hit and fell right where he was standing. A Soldier, who went by the name of Tiny (6 feet 5 inches) and
a battle buddy jumped down and picked him up. Just by
glancing at him they knew it was a near hopeless case to
save him. The medics were not near, and a dressing station was not close by. Grabbing some empty sand bags
and an old coat, they laid the wounded soldier in the bottom of the trench. Back on the firing step, Tiny and his
battle buddy continued to hold the line.

A few minutes later Tiny heard a voice behind him,

"Can you tell me the way to heaven?"

Tiny jumped back down in the trench and asked, "The way to heaven? I'm sorry I don't know the way, but I'll ask the other fellas and find out if they know."

Returning to the firing step, Tiny commenced walking along and asked the first soldier, but he didn't know. So, he went further and asked the next man, but he didn't know either. Tiny went over to the next fire bay and asked the fourth man, but he was not help either. From there, one by one, each man asked the next if they knew the way to heaven? Down the line the story went until it reached the 16th man and still, no one could tell the way to heaven. Just think of it!

Young men growing up in a so-called Christian land, but they couldn't help their dying comrade.

When you have soldiered together, gone overseas together, and faced the dangers and hardships of active service, you become buddies. When you see an old friend dying you want to give them the real thing, not some quick answer to pacify. Could you have told this dying soldier the way to heaven? Can you open the Bible and point out God's way to heaven?

Now, back to the trench–The story is passed to soldier number 17. "Sam is dying and wants to know the way to heaven. Can you tell him the way?"

Turning around and with a smile lighting up his face, he replied, "Yes, I know the way to heaven, but I can't leave my station." Pulling a small New Testament from his pocket, he turned its pages and said, "Look here, this is the way to heaven—that verse circled in pencil (John 3:16). Tell him that's the way to heaven."

Quickly the message and the Testament passed back from man to man until it reached Tiny. He touched his comrade's shoulder and slowly Sam opened his eyes. "I've got it old chum," said Tiny, "Here's the way to heaven:

"For God so loved the world that he gave His only Son, and whosoever believes in him, shall not perish, but have everlasting life."

With poor Sam's eyes wide open taking in every word, and Tiny kneeling beside him in the trench, he said, "Read it again".

So, with tears running down his face, Tiny read the life-giving Words over and over. A look of peace came over Sam's countenance as he kept gasping out, "Whosoever". Then after lying quietly; his face lit up with satisfaction and with one last gasp he said, "Whosoever, that means me," and then he was gone.

Sam had found the way to heaven, because someone knew the way and told him how. We must be ready, willing, and able to share the way. We mustn't hinder the progress of the gospel. People's lives and souls are depending on it.

Three ways we can promote the gospel: 1) Don't hold it down—lift it up (Psalm 20:5). Some people stifle the growth of the Kingdom because they fail to accept their share of responsibility. Our world is desperately searching for something to satisfy the longing soul. We must work together in unity and lift high the banner of salvation; 2) Don't hold it in—let it out (Luke 9:26). Some fail to witness for Christ because they are self-conscious. We must become God-conscious. He will supply the needed strength and courage. No one group of Christians has a corner on salvation. The gospel is not for any exclusive individual, group, or denomination. It is for "Whosoever "believeth; 3) Don't hold it back—launch it forth (Mark 13:10). All Christians can send forth the gospel through preparation and prayer. Distance is no problem with God. Millions of people can be reached through churches, the printed page, digital platforms, and good old-fashioned word-of-mouth.

Know the gospel and promote it! Romans 1:16-17 says, ***"For I am not ashamed of this Good News about Christ. It is the power of God at work, saving everyone who believes. The Good News tells us how God makes us right in His sight. This*** *is accomplished from start to finish by faith. It is through faith that a person has life".*

245

<u>How to Tell the Good News</u>

- ♦ Don't Hold It Down—Lift it Up!

- ♦ Don't Hold It In—Let It Out!

- ♦ Don't Hold It Back—Launch It Forth!

EPILOGUE

This book is my fifth volume of the Living With Purpose series. I anticipate others in the future, if it be God's will. But, if this is to be the last, I am confident there is enough content and guidance from Scripture contained within this one to lead you home to glory! Embrace the words of our Lord and Savior Jesus Christ and hopefully, in some small way, my words have encouraged you also.

R. Matthew Dobson

January 1, 2020

Jay, Florida

ABOUT THE AUTHOR

This is the fifth volume in the Living With Purpose book series written by Dobson. His inspirational writing draws from life experiences and his personal pursuit of positive living. He challenges you to look for the good in all things and make life worth living for yourself and those around you.

www.ingramcontent.com/pod-product-compliance
Lightning Source LLC
Chambersburg PA
CBHW020323160726
47992CB00004B/1672